CHIEF WILLIAM McINTOSH

A MAN OF TWO WORLDS

CHIEF WILLIAM MCINTOSH

A MAN OF TWO WORLDS

BY GEORGE CHAPMAN

Illustrations by John Kollock

Cherokee Publishing Company
Atlanta, Georgia
1988

Library of Congress Cataloging-in-Publication Data

Chapman, George, 1928–
　Chief William McIntosh　:　a man of two worlds.

　Bibliography:　p.
　Includes index.
　1. McIntosh, William, ca. 1775–1825.　2. Creek Indians—Biogra-
phy.　3. Creek Indians—History.　4. Indians of North America—Geor-
gia—Biography.　5. Indians of North America—Georgia—History.
I. Title.
E99.C9M383　　　1988　　　975.8′00497　[B]　　　　　88-11872
ISBN 0-87797-133-1 (alk. paper)

This book is printed on acid-free paper which conforms to the American
National Standard Z39.48-1984 *Permanence of Paper for Printed Library
Materials*. Paper that conforms to this standard's requirements for pH,
alkaline reserve and freedom from groundwood is anticipated to last several hundred years without significant deterioration under normal library
use and storage conditions. ⊗

Manufactured in the United States of America
First Edition
ISBN: 0-87797-133-1

97　96　95　94　93　92　91　90　89　88　　　10　9　8　7　6　5　4　3　2　1
Edited by Alexa Selph
Design by Paulette Lambert

Cherokee Publishing Company is an operating division of
the Larlin Corporation, PO Box 1730, Marietta, GA 30061

CONTENTS

ILLUSTRATIONS

ACKNOWLEDGMENTS

I owe a debt of gratitude to the McIntosh family, the descendants of Chief William McIntosh, for their friendship, support, and information on Creek tradition that is not available in written form. Chief (Ret.) Waldo E. "Dode" McIntosh, five times principal chief of the Creek Indian Nation, has sent materials about family and Creek history that cannot be found in libraries. Dode's son Chinnubbie has shared oral tradition concerning the ancient ceremonies and dances of the Creeks. Mrs. Wilfred M. Lee, Dode's daughter, has given her friendship and her support.

I am deeply indebted to the late Dr. James C. Bonner, professor emeritus of history, Georgia College in Milledgeville, who read an early draft and the final draft of the manuscript. He offered valuable suggestions concerning historical perspectives. Dr. Bonner encouraged me, without knowing it, to write the book. Appreciation is also expressed to Franklin Garrett, emeritus historian of the Atlanta Historical Society, for reading an early draft and offering stylistic and historical suggestions. I also want to thank Mrs. Carolyn Cary, historian of Fayette County, for reading the manuscript and making suggestions.

Thanks to my wife and best friend, Shirley, a homegrown editor whose instinct for good reading is usually right. Her suggestions were very helpful.

Appreciation is expressed to Paul Ghioto, park historian, Horseshoe Bend National Military Park, for a copy of Swan's record of his visit to the Creek Nation in 1791. I am indebted to the late Bessie Lewis, historian of McIntosh County, for helping with information about William McIntosh's early life.

Thanks to the staffs of the following libraries: Atlanta-Fulton Public Library, Georgia Department of Archives and History, Georgia State University, Emory University, National Library of Scotland, Edinburgh, Scotland, and the University of Georgia; the staffs of the following were also helpful: Georgia Historical Society; National Archives, Washington, D.C.; and the Bureau of Indian Affairs, Washington, D.C.

PREFACE

In the fall of 1969 I resigned my job as manager of a radio station in Decatur, Georgia, to pursue an ambition that I had had for a long time. Having been clinically trained as a pastoral counselor, I wanted updated training in mental health, so I enrolled as a graduate student in psychology at West Georgia College in Carrollton, Georgia.

As I walked around the campus, I felt excitement about pursuing a master's degree in psychology and anxiety about long-unused study habits. The trees around the new psychology building and the carpeted halls inside contributed to the old library hush. Knowledge was hallowed here.

For the first week of classes I dressed in my usual business suit, while the rest of the student body wore jeans. I soon adopted their uniform and became reasonably accepted. From one of the students I heard a rumor about a treasure, buried, supposedly nearby, by an Indian. From my days as a Boy Scout I had developed an interest in the American Indian, so the student and I decided to go looking for the treasure in our spare time. On his instructions I drove to the McIntosh Reserve, about four miles west of Whitesburg, in Carroll County, Georgia. There I found a large, pine-studded knoll beside the Chattahoochee River, where the Creek Indian Chief William McIntosh had lived and where he had been assassinated. Rumors had spread that he had stashed a treasure somewhere on the reserve.

As I thought of the treasure, I developed a plan to scan the area with a metal detector. Several current treasure magazines and a book about local treasures indicated that the McIntosh cache was in gold coin; therefore, a detector would find it. Yet, as I looked at the land, overgrown with thickets and tall grass, I knew that it would take a week of clearing before a detector could be used there. Besides, we had not received permission to do the search, an absolute must on others' property.

Our ardor for the search was cooled by these obstacles and by the hours of demanding graduate study. Three years later I earned my degree, began looking for a job, and resumed historical research on the treasure. The magazines and the book calculated the treasure at $500,000, paid to McIntosh when he signed the treaty of 1825. Careful research (in this case, reading the actual treaty) showed this to be in error. First of all, the amount in question was $400,000, not $500,000; it was to be paid to the entire Creek Nation, and McIntosh was to receive a chief's share. The treaty was later nullified by the incoming U.S. president, John Quincy Adams. I ultimately concluded that there was no treasure and that Chief William McIntosh, a talented and adventurous man, was caught in a web of historical controversy that eventually cost him his life.

This is his story, and herein lies the real treasure.

I

The Birth of McIntosh

RUDYARD Kipling, the poet-adventurer, noting the vast cultural differences between England and India, wrote, "East is east, and west is west, and never the twain shall meet."[1] Kipling, however, did not know Chief William McIntosh, who was born into the two worlds of the Highland Scot and the Creek Indian Nation.

The meeting of diverse cultures was inevitable as European kingdoms enjoyed a renaissance of the arts, literature, and competitive exploration of the new world. In the early eighteenth century Alexander Pope wrote his famous *Essay on Man*, Johann Sebastian Bach composed his *Mass in B Minor*, and Spain, England, and France were fighting one another for territory in the new world. James E. Oglethorpe founded Savannah and brought a group of emigrant Highland Scots to defend the new colony against Spanish aggression. One of the soldiers in that group was John McIntosh, an emigrant from Borlum, Scotland.[2] John had a son, William, who as a boy, played with young Indians at Darien, in the colony of Georgia. During his teenage years William fought side-by-side with the Creek warriors, defending colonial Georgia against Spanish aggression.[3]

Later, John McIntosh and his family moved to a frontier home called McIntosh Bluffs, on the Tombigbee River, above Mobile, in what is now Alabama.[4] There William, now a captain in the colonial army, met and married Senoia Henneha, of whom little is known.[5] She was perhaps the daughter of the chief (micco, or king) of Cow-

13

eta-Cussetta towns, of the Lower Creeks. These towns were located on both sides of the Chattahoochee River, in present-day Georgia and Alabama. Coweta was located just below what is now the city of Columbus, on the west bank of the Chattahoochee, and Cussetta was a few miles south of Coweta, on the east bank of the Chatta-hoochee.[6] Senoia was a member of the aristocratic Wind clan. It is possible that the town of Senoia, in Coweta County, Georgia, was named for her.

Her son William McIntosh was born about 1775, near We-tumpka, Georgia (now Alabama).[7] At that time the territory of Georgia extended from the Atlantic Ocean to the Mississippi River. In addition to William, his father had another son, Roley (about four years younger than the chief), by his second wife. Roley's mother may have been of the same tribe and clan as Senoia.

Little is known of William's early life. As he grew, he was taught to speak both Muscogee—the language of the Muscogee, or Creek, Indians—and English. During the American Revolution, his father probably brought British officers to the Creek Nation to show them the frontier and life among the Indians. William would use the opportunity to converse in English. Between military engagements during the long war, William's father spent time at home with his families. The young Indian enjoyed the strong, tender hugs of his father and the manly warmth of his eyes. He loved his father's joy of life, his daring, and the commanding way he walked and lived. Sometimes William would catch his mother's eye as she looked at her husband. She would smile, and pride would fill the young Indi-an's heart. He wanted more than anything else to be like his father and, from an early age, wanted to become a warrior.

McIntosh understood the language of the traders and the gov-ernment officials, and he would explain to the Creek chiefs what he had heard. Although he was bilingual from an early age, McIntosh learned to write English later as an adult.

By tribal custom William's uncles on his mother's side had more to say about his training than did his father.[8] An uncle, Coweta Micco, probably taught young William and his half brother, Roley, how to hunt for game. They went into the forest, looking for rabbit, fox, and deer. They ate the meat and wore the animals' fur. Micco

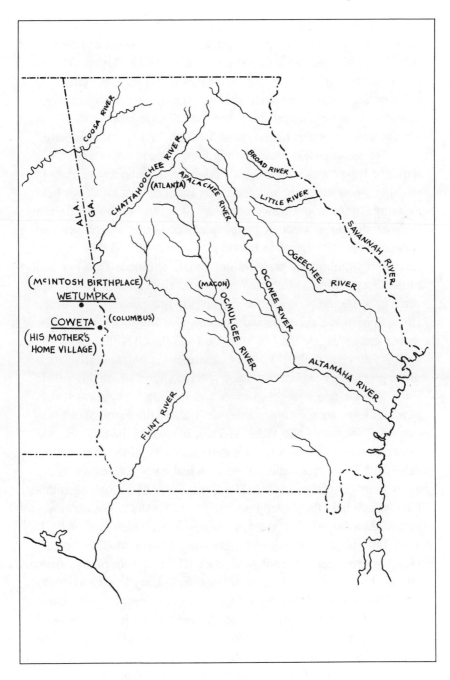

The area where McIntosh's mother was from, and the area where he was born.

taught them the patience required for fishing on the river for food. As William grew, he ran the distance between Coweta and Broken Arrow and felt the increasing strength in his body. During the heat of the summer months he wore a loincloth, and his skin turned the color of the earth. Summer's warmth allowed swimming in rivers whose waters were dangerous when the alligators appeared. It was not unusual for bodies to disappear between the jaws of a predator.[9]

The summer was also the time for the green corn dance. William and Roley would sit and watch their uncles join the warriors in stacking wood into a mound. Then, by tradition that no longer held meaning, the warriors would chase any dogs from the area.[10] Each summer the boys watched as the warriors lit the sacred fire and danced to the left in a circle around it. They chanted as they danced, and the rhythm put the warriors in a hypnotic mood. They reached to the Great Spirit as they danced around the sacred fire. William came to sense the power in the fire and, in that power, life. For the Great Spirit gave the sun, and the sun gave life to the earth. The sacred fire embodied the life of the sun and the Great Spirit.

As they grew older, William and Roley caught the festive spirit of the green corn celebration. Each received a pair of leggings made from deerskin and a jacket to cover him in winter. They watched as new buildings were painted in new colors and the mood of celebration filled the towns and villages. Their uncle told the boys that the ancient towns of Coweta and Cussetta had first joined in a pact for defense.[11] The Creeks and other tribes had early formed a confederacy that was still powerful. The Great Spirit had given them this land, which held the sacred bones of their ancestors. The earth was part of their bodies and bones, a giant skin on which they walked. They felt its pulse and its life. It brought forth food and game, yielding trees, berries, fruit, and roots. The Great Spirit, the uncle told the boys, gave its children of the forest plenty to eat and drink.

The climax of the festival was the great feast of green corn, prepared by the women and eaten in the town square. The boys enjoyed the spirit of fun, festivity, and the religious fervor and communion that prevailed. The festival evoked a spirit of power and invincibility, prosperity, and abundance. The ritual of the green corn festival was a ceremonial affirmation of these joys.

One day Coweta Micco told the boys about the Wind clan. Their members, he said, were often tribal leaders.[12] Other clans had a statute of limitations on pursuing persons who had committed crimes against them, but the Wind clan had none. The chief looked out across the river, where the fog occasionally gathered, and told the tribal legend. William and Roley listened to every word.

In ancient times, he began, a fog came upon the land and the people walked in darkness. Families were separated and everyone was afraid. When any two persons touched, they clung together until another joined and they grew into large groups. Animals, too, were afraid of the darkness and joined the people. Finally, a wind blew the fog away, and the first clan to emerge became the Wind clan, recognized as the leading clan because it first saw the light.[13]

The boys also heard tales of their Indian past told by the medicine men and chiefs and performed by ceremonial dancers who reenacted the military victories of the Creeks. They also called to the rain clouds during planting seasons and spread their arms in the ceremonial flight of the thunderbird.

They learned from nature her songs and moods, carried by her winds as they walked the ancient paths through the forests. Carefully, William and Roley watched, learning to read the changing seasons and the times of planting and harvesting. As they watched clouds and rain, sunshine and occasional snow, and felt the warmth and the cold, they came to know the Great Spirit who gave them.

After he had passed ten summers at Coweta, William began to spend more time listening to warriors and chiefs. He learned to read the silence of old warriors, who felt passionately but seldom spoke.

As the seasons passed, William and Roley grew toward warriorhood. Roley, who now stood just a few inches short of William, heard the call of the forest. William heard that call but also felt drawn to the white man's world. In his blood flowed both worlds. His thoughts moved easily from the world of the Creeks to the world of the whites. William's skin was lighter than that of his Indian brothers. He remembered his father's ways and thoughts, different from those of his mother and the chiefs. The cultural differences between the two worlds were becoming more and more evident.

Because the white man's world was infringing more and more

Coweta Micco tells the boys about the Wind clan.

on Indian territory and thought, the chiefs considered William's ability an asset. Maybe the young McIntosh could help them to better understand the white man, who had come across the ocean. The chiefs kept their eyes on this young man who stood out in abilities among the youths.

About the time William reached his early teens his father made a big decision. As Harriet Corbin, in her book *A History and Genealogy of Chief William McIntosh, Jr.,* wrote,

> Captain William thought his two sons were ready for more formal education (so) he talked to his Indian wives about sending them to Scotland for a period. Now, this was not a matter for a fast decision, their tribal rules governing the sons of these Indian mothers. The brothers of the Indian mothers had more to say about what was done with the boys than their own father. The uncles were not at all in favor of having these two members of the tribe sent out of the country for any reason. After due time, it was agreed that the boys could go to Scotland, but that their mothers were to remain home for security. This would assure that the sons returned to the Creek Nation.
>
> It was a long trip to the coast for the two boys to board the ship, and they were very tired when they got on board. The boys were placed in their bunks, and Captain McIntosh joined the other passengers in the lounge. Later in the evening, when the captain returned to his stateroom, the boys were missing. He learned that, in his absence, the uncles had come aboard and gained custody of the youngsters and had taken them ashore. Nothing could be done about it now for the ship was at sea and the captain was taking the trip alone.[14]

A few years after that voyage William's father decided to leave his Indian families, and he returned to the coast. When this happened, the marriage was considered "broken" (divorced). As a reward for his military service he was awarded land—Fair Hope, on the Sapelo River, and Mallow, just north of it (located in present-day McIntosh County).[15] The Captain married a cousin, Barbara McIntosh, and they made their home at Mallow.

William and Roley continued their woodland education in Creek ancestral customs, under the guiding hands of their uncles. They learned the pride of being in the Wind clan. They learned the age-old art of making arrows, spears, and tomahawks. They learned to shoot rifles and they hunted for deer. They were also taught to skin an animal. From the first deer that William shot, his mother made a buckskin outfit for him. It fitted well and made him look like a warrior.

William McIntosh's frame soon passed the six-foot mark. He had learned to ride a horse and often traveled to Mallow to see his father. He enjoyed the company of his Scottish relatives, whose zest for life embodied the spirit of the frontier. His father had built a sturdy home, which William liked, and the Indian determined that one day he would build one for himself. He noted that the houses kept out the cold winter wind. Colonial homes had wooden floors rather than the earthen ones found in most Indian homes. He peered curiously through the windows at moss-draped oaks.

William's father, in their talks, often recalled his early years. William's favorite story was about how the Creek warriors had fought in the Revolution. The captain's eyes, framed by gray sideburns, would assume a faraway look. "I played with Indian boys when I was young," he began in a Highland burr. "They knew the forests, for it was their home. Weather didn't bother them. I have never seen such a hardy breed. They were the best of friends. When I grew older, fighting with the Spaniards broke out again. I hid with the Indians, without my father knowing about it. I was a battle veteran when I was your age. I fought with the Creeks and saw my father—your grandfather—taken prisoner by the Spanish." Then he added, with a smile, "They were as fierce as the Scots." William knew that his father could pay them no higher compliment.

When William was about nineteen years old, his father died and was buried among the graves of the Scots, around the "Great Oak" tree, a huge oak at Mallow.[16] The young McIntosh came to the coast to pay tribute to his father, who was now resting in the earth

William in his deerskin outfit.

he had fought to win. Having bidden farewell to his father's widow and family, William took back to Coweta, as his inheritance, several horses that his father had owned.

William McIntosh had a strong sense of honor and dignity. His personality was commanding. His eyes—stern and piercing—missed nothing. The dark hair and eyes of his Indian heritage were softened by the relatively light skin of his Scottish blood. It is likely that his leadership potential was recognized early, as his authoritative manner began to assert itself. In the tradition of the Creeks, he probably led war parties into enemy villages to make a name for himself as a warrior. It was after William had returned from such a skirmish that Coweta honored him as a warrior.[17] He was given a personal name—Tustunuge Hutke (Tustunnuggee), meaning "White Warrior."[18]

When William was about twenty-five, he was chosen as a chief of Coweta town. Coweta was one of four "mother" towns on which the Creek Indian Nation had been founded.[19] The others were Cussetta, Osweechee, and Tuckabatchee. Coweta and Cussetta both claimed to be older than the rest, but Cussetta's tradition as the oldest was recognized by the chiefs of the Indian Confederacy. Coweta's territory lay on both sides of the Chattahoochee River, reaching north from Broken Arrow (about eight miles below present-day Phenix City, Alabama), to Cherokee territory.[20] It was the largest in the nation in both size and population.[21] As one of its chiefs, William McIntosh inherited honor, an ancient authority over other chiefs, and royal standing as a member of the Wind clan.

About this time Chief William married Eliza Grierson, a mixed-blood daughter of Robert Grierson.[22] Grierson was a Scottish trader, well-known in the Creek nation. McIntosh built a home for his bride on the Tallapoosa River, fifty miles west of present-day Whitesburg, Georgia. A son, Chilly, was born to them about 1800. Two daughters—Jane and Kate—followed. Eliza was soon busy, raising a growing family. Chief McIntosh began his children's education by teaching them to speak both Muscogee and English. Like their father, they were born into two worlds.

During the decade before McIntosh became a chief, the lead-

ership of the Indian Confederacy had changed. Alexander Mc-
Gillivray, the former principal chief of the Creek Nation, had been
"broken" (fired) because he had signed an unpopular treaty. He died
in Pensacola, Florida. Little Prince, an aged and venerated warrior,
emerged as the new principal chief. His skin was the color of the
earth, and his face was as lined as old parchment. The old chief was
an admirer and supporter of McIntosh.[23] Big Warrior (Tustennuggee
Thlucco) became principal chief of the Upper Towns. He lived at
Tuckabatchee, on the Coosa River. The warrior who became War
Chief of the Upper Towns was Menawa (Ogillis Incha), chief of the
Hillabee villages. His reputation as a do-or-die daredevil came from
his exploits on the Tennessee frontier, where he stole horses from
settlers. His bravery brought him startled admiration, even homage,
from the warriors. Like McIntosh, he was of mixed blood, but he
had no regard for the white man. When McIntosh was elected a
chief of the Lower Towns, word of his abilities passed from town to
town across the Creek Nation. When it reached the ear of Menawa,
a frown knotted over his sharp black eyes. Menawa's suspicion of
McIntosh was indicative of the Upper and Lower Towns' growing
polarity concerning culture, race, religion, and the economy.[24]

The Indians, drawn by the economy of the colonists, moved
their towns closer to the coast.[25] The Creeks seemed to favor the
leadership of mixed-blood Indians, such as Chief McIntosh. Speaking the languages of both cultures and feeling a sense of heritage
from both the Creeks and the whites, mixed-bloods often moved
more easily in the two worlds than did their full-blooded brothers.

The Lower Creeks, such as Chief McIntosh, accepted Christian missions as a way of strengthening the Creeks. The Upper Town
chiefs, such as Menawa, saw them as tools for the white man's
subjugation of the Indian. Some of McIntosh's children became
Baptists, probably because of Withington, a Baptist mission from
the North in the territory of the Lower Towns.

The Lower Towns were attracted to the economy of the whites,
trading furs for hunting rifles, knives, farming implements, apparel,
and jewelry. When war broke out between the Creeks and the English, the Creeks retreated to the former site of their towns. Later,

as treaties for land were signed, money, in the form of annuities, began to replace skins and other trade items used by the Indians. The Creeks were drawn into the government economy.

Chief McIntosh grew up in an age when the United States considered the Creeks a "protectorate" because they had fought on the side of the British during the Revolution. Deer had become scarce, so the Indians were depending more and more on government annuities for trading power, and land was becoming the main instrument of barter.

II

The Red Sticks' War
1813–14

HAVING recovered from a hard-fought revolution, the United States began to plan expansion to territories west, toward the Mississippi River. By the treaty of Fort Wilkerson, in 1802, the United States purchased Georgia's claim to all territories in present-day Alabama and Mississippi, and all Indian land in Georgia. The treaty enabled the new government to gain a foothold on the west bank of the Oconee River, near present-day Milledgeville, Georgia. The United States now owned all the coast of Georgia and inland as far as Milledgeville. Then, in 1803 the United States purchased the territory of Louisiana from France, cutting off further wilderness retreat by the Upper Creeks, who had pushed westward to find more game. Buffalo and deer were hard to find on the coast, forcing the Indians to look for other sources of meat. All that remained were wild turkey, foxes, and rabbits. The tribes were feeling cramped for space, and resentment toward white settlers was spreading rapidly among the Indians.

Ignoring the dwindling food supply of the tribes, President Thomas Jefferson ordered Indian Agent Benjamin Hawkins to bring chiefs and headmen of the Creek Nation to Washington to negotiate for land on the Ocmulgee River near present-day Macon, Georgia. The president wanted to create a horse path from the Ocmulgee to Fort Stoddart, near present-day Mobile, Alabama, so that settlers could travel more easily.

Chief William McIntosh and Indian Interpreter Alexander Cornells, who were among the chiefs selected by Agent Hawkins, were the best known of the delegation. The party traveled through Sparta and Augusta, Georgia, then to Washington for deliberations with Secretary of War Henry Dearborn. Talks began on November 14, 1803, with the white ruffled shirt and tailored black suit of the secretary contrasting with the more primitive frontier style of the chiefs, who wore buckskin leggings, brass earrings, and white feathers in their hair as a symbol of peace. On official occasions such as this, McIntosh would wear a shirt with his buckskin pants and his chief's turban with its plumed feather.

The chiefs listened to Dearborn's proposals for the treaty. The United States wanted land on the Oconee River, between present-day Macon and Milledgeville, and land on the Ocmulgee River. The Ocmulgee flows through Macon and by the Old Ocmulgee Fields, which were sacred to the Creeks. The secretary explained that the United States wanted to cut a horse path from the Ocmulgee River to Mobile to allow greater westward movement of settlers and travelers.

McIntosh understood Dearborn's proposals in English, and he watched the secretary's stern expression as he outlined the treaty. The chief felt that the United States was demanding the land, not bartering for it, and that the demand for a horse path was unreasonable. His spirit braced as he thought of losing the sacred ground at Ocmulgee. As Timothy Barnard, the Scottish interpreter, carefully explained the points of the treaty to the chiefs, McIntosh and Cornells listened intently. The chiefs reacted quickly: they did not like the idea of a horse path and believed that it would allow too many settlers access to land west of the Chattahoochee River. Many settlers had already built cabins along the rivers in frontier Alabama and Mississippi. The Creek delegation decided against the proposal, and Barnard communicated their refusal to the secretary. Dearborn, however, remained adamant. New laws could be written, he explained, to protect both Indians and whites.

After a few minutes of silence, the chiefs repeated their strong objections to the treaty proposals. Then McIntosh spoke in English to the secretary, emphasizing the Creeks' beliefs that the rivers already provided food and transportation and that the existing paths were sufficient. The proposed horse path, McIntosh offered, would

McIntosh and the other chiefs meet with Secretary of War Dearborn.

bring conflict between Indians and whites. Dearborn, however, would not be moved. Because the United States was the stronger power, a feeling of resignation swept over the chiefs. The treaty was signed that day.[1]

Afterward, Chief McIntosh remarked to Cornells and Barnard that the United States government seemed never to be satisfied with the land it had. With this treaty, the government now possessed nearly one-third of the state of Georgia.

The horse path, originally designed to begin on the Ocmulgee River, began instead at Fort Wilkerson on the Oconee River and extended to Fort Stoddart at Mobile. From four to six feet wide, the path soon carried settlers in wagons and on horseback in a steady stream to frontier territory. Then, in 1811, Lieutenant Luckett, commanding a party of soldiers, cut the path called the Federal Road, from the Chattahoochee River to Mims' Ferry on the Alabama River.[2] Warriors chafed at the numerous settlements that were springing up along the rivers. Too many people meant too little game.

. . .

On August 5, 1811, a Shawnee chief named Tecumseh and his band of twenty warriors came to Tuckabatchee, the capital of the Indian Confederacy. Tecumseh wanted the southern tribes to band together and run the white man off the tribal lands forever.[3] They arrived in time for the Creek National Council, where the nation's business was conducted each year.

When all tribal business had been tended to and Agent Hawkins had left, Tecumseh was presented to the chiefs and the headmen. McIntosh had been asked by Hawkins to report on the council's reactions to the Shawnee chief. McIntosh and the assembled chiefs watched Tecumseh as he prayed to the Great Spirit. As Tecumseh moved about the council, his cousin Seekaboo interpreted for him. Tecumseh walked with a limp, but it was soon forgotten as Seekaboo translated his words and feelings.

McIntosh noted the red and white feathers rising from the Shawnee's headband. The white feather symbolized peace toward his Indian brothers; the red feather stood for war on all whites. His

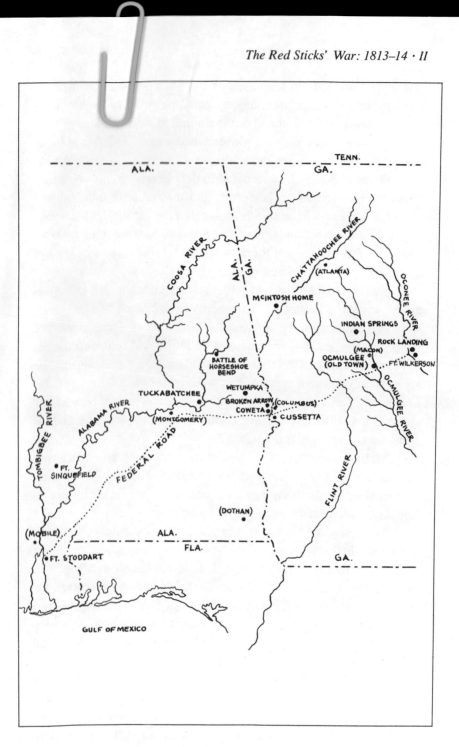

The federal road (horse path) and Indian towns.

dark eyes fastened on Tecumseh as the Shawnee's eloquent voice
and hypnotic facial expressions appealed powerfully to the Indian
heart, a call-to-arms to the aboriginal mind to save the land of their
fathers. Then Chief William glanced at the other chiefs and headmen in the council. Every eye was on Tecumseh, as he spoke out
loud the feelings they had harbored in their hearts. In his voice they
heard the free winds of the forest, and the Indians' mystical past
blazed in his eyes. Tecumseh mesmerized the braves with a strong
call to fight for their lands, now being wrenched from them by land-
hungry whites. He urged them to kill the domestic cows they had
adopted from the "civilized world."

Chief McIntosh listened with growing concern. He knew that
many warriors, frustrated by settlers who hunted scarce game,
would be swayed by the Shawnee. He listened as Tecumseh urged
them to throw away their store-bought plows and return to the old
days when game and corn were plentiful and life was beautiful. He
spoke fondly of summers, when he would return to his former home
to hunt and participate in religious festivals, and he told how he had
come to know the Great Spirit. Until the closing word, he had the
attention of everyone present.

McIntosh and the other chiefs then watched as the twenty warriors who rode with Tecumseh performed the Dance of the Lakes.
The frenzied rhythm gave powerful impetus to the Shawnee's emo-
tional talk and became an anthem of rebellion.

Tecumseh and his warriors remained at Tuckabatchee for about
a week while the Shawnee talked with McIntosh and the other chiefs
and headmen of the Confederacy. He talked at length with Big Warrior, the big, pock-faced chief from Tuckabatchee, who received the
peace pipe and the bundle of red sticks from Tecumseh. Big Warrior
was to throw away one stick each day until all were gone, at which
time the Creeks, in concert with all other tribes, were to attack all
white settlements and towns. Big Warrior, however, did not commit
himself to a war of rebellion. Nor did Little Prince, the principal
chief of the Creek Nation, accept Tecumseh's talk. Instead, he held
to the peace with the federal government that had been established
by the treaty of 1790. The War Chief Menawa, although strongly
attracted to the emotionally persuasive Tecumseh, would not com-

mit himself. Chief McIntosh listened carefully to the Shawnee's appeal for a confederacy that would make war for freedom. He also remembered his father's stories about fighting the rebel colonies. Part of him liked Tecumseh's talk, but part of him rebelled against it. The United States had grown strong, probably too strong for the Indian nations. McIntosh decided to accept neither Tecumseh's talk nor his peace pipe.

Agent Hawkins had asked Chief McIntosh and Big Warrior to tell him what Tecumseh had said, and after the national council ended, Chief William returned to Coweta and described the reactions of the chiefs and the headmen to Tecumseh's talk. Although Hawkins apparently did not consider the Shawnee a serious threat to peace, many of the warriors had been fired with the spirit of rebellion as they listened to Tecumseh's fervid call to arms.

On March 26, 1812, drunken Indians from Autassee, a sacred war village in the Upper Towns, killed a white man, Thomas Meredith, and his family at Kittome.[4] A couple of months later William Lott, a pioneer on his way to the Mississippi frontier, was killed by a large band of Tallisee Indians of the Upper Creeks.[5] Then, two families on the Duck River in Tennessee were killed by warriors from the Hillabee village of the Upper Creeks. Alexander Cornells reported to Agent Hawkins that the killings had occurred without provocation and that settlers in Tennessee had grown both fearful and resentful of the frontier incidents.

Agent Hawkins sent for Chief McIntosh, and they went together to see Little Prince to discuss what could be done. The old chief, concerned by the disturbing developments in the Creek Nation, sent them to Menawa. The War Chief of the Upper Towns headed the Hillabee villages. The chief's face, scarred by smallpox, grew red as he confronted McIntosh. He gave in to Agent Hawkins' counsel, however, and put Chief McIntosh in charge of a contingent of warriors from Coweta, Cussetta, and Tuckabatchee.

Chief McIntosh and the warriors went in search of the offenders to administer justice. In a few weeks they had caught six ringleaders, who were then shot.[6] Others were caught and whipped. This retaliatory action was meant to teach the lawbreakers a lesson and discourage further incidents. The action, however, only provoked a greater tension between the chiefs of the Upper and the Lower Towns.[7] It angered Tecumseh's converts and their relatives, and the chiefs began to realize the extent of Tecumseh's influence. More warriors than they had thought were in his sway.

Big Warrior feared the "war party," which was now growing in number and influence every day. The rebel Indians vowed to destroy Chief McIntosh, Big Warrior, Little Prince, and all those connected with the killings.[8]

Tecumseh's careful, persistent influence had reached into the ranks of the chiefs. Succumbing to calculated persuasion, Menawa joined the rebels, most of whom were from towns under his leadership.

In July of 1812, Lateau, an eighteen-year-old Indian who claimed to be a prophet of the rebels, gathered eight followers and went to the old town of Coosa. There, after performing the Dance of the Lakes for a gathering of friendly chiefs, they killed three of them. The chiefs who escaped returned with their own warriors and executed the young prophet and his followers. The chiefs then went to Little Oakfuskee and killed other followers of Tecumseh.

Enraged by these retaliations, the rebel Creeks announced their intention to attack Tuckabatchee, the capital. On hearing this, Big Warrior and other chiefs of that town immediately fortified it and sent to the Lower Towns for help. Chief McIntosh and Joseph Marshall of the Coweta towns and Chief Timpoochee Barnard of the Uchees selected two hundred warriors and responded to the call for help. They went to the capital and escorted the inhabitants to Coweta for safety. The rebels attacked both Tuckabatchee and Kialigie, ancient towns known to be friendly with the white man. The towns had felt secure in the past, for they had never before been attacked. The Creek Nation was shocked.

Agent Hawkins became sick about this time and could not go to the rebels to persuade them to stop. Thinking that the Creeks would fight only among themselves, he assured General Ferdinand Claiborne of the United States Army and General John Floyd of the Georgia militia that they need not be concerned. Hawkins said that the Creeks had reached a high degree of civilization and had peaceful intentions toward the whites.

Tecumseh returned north to the Shawnee Nation, and his converts formed bands that roamed the countryside, demanding that all Creeks join their holy war against the whites. Prophet Joseph Francis, High-Head Jim, and Peter McQueen, the leaders of the rebel Indians, went to Spanish-held Pensacola for guns and ammunition. While there, they performed the war dance, a declaration of war against the whites. The rebels, now called "Red Sticks," planned to distribute ammunition among the warriors and attack settlers. (*Red Sticks* probably stood for war clubs, which were painted red, the color of war.[9])

Colonel James Caller, commanding a contingent of militia, under orders from Mississippi Governor Don Manique, attacked the Red Sticks at Burnt Corn Creek. These rebels were preparing to attack white settlers. The result was a rout; the militia fled the battle area. The rebels suddenly felt invincible against the white oppressor. Chiefs and headmen who had hesitated to join Tecumseh now swelled the rebels' ranks. In retaliation for the Burnt Corn surprise battle, the Red Sticks attacked Fort Mims on August 30, 1813. The gate of the fort was left open by a drunken Major Beasley, who was killed by warriors as they charged in to attack. Over five hundred soldiers, men, women, children, Negroes, friendly Creeks, and deserting Spaniards, died in that battle.

More confident of their war-making powers, the rebels moved to attack Fort Sinquefield. The settlers' war hysteria had risen to fever pitch. Whites and friendly Creeks gathered within the protective walls of the fort. The dress of the attacking rebels was similar to that of Tecumseh's warriors. To scare the enemy, they painted their faces with red paint, a symbol of war, and bound their heads with turkey feathers to resemble a flock of birds. The Red Sticks attacked Fort Sinquefield with strength and fury, but this time the soldiers and the settlers in the fort were ready. The battle raged for several hours. The rebels maintained a continual fire from behind trees and stumps, as well as from the windows of an abandoned house nearby. The soldiers and the settlers returned the fire from portholes in the walls of the fort. About two o'clock in the afternoon the fighting ended, the Red Sticks having lost eleven men, the settlers, two.

As the news of the Red Sticks' attacks on Fort Mims and Fort Sinquefield reached Washington, the young capital responded with rage. In July 1813 the United States Congress authorized a force of three thousand militiamen under General John Floyd of Georgia, and the East and Middle Divisions of Tennessee under General John White to move against the Red Sticks. Also under orders was the lesser-known Brigadier General Andrew Jackson of the Second Division, who raised an army of volunteers. He also recruited a detachment of friendly Creeks, Cherokees, Chickasaws, and Choctaws under Chief Pushmata.[10] The massacre at Fort Mims, more than the previous battle at Burnt Corn Creek, signaled the entrance of the United States into the Red Sticks' war.

Chief William McIntosh, commissioned a major by Agent Hawkins, was to lead a contingent of warriors. The chief remembered the warriors whom he had led while bringing the people from Tuckabatchee to Coweta and chose them to join the ranks. Also commissioned was Timpoochee Barnard, a chief of the Uchees. Like McIntosh, he was the son of a Scottish father and an Indian mother.

McIntosh said farewell to his wife, Eliza, and their thirteen-year-old son, Chilly, who had learned to make arrows and now carried a hunting knife. Chilly wanted to go with his father, but the chief gently admonished him to wait a few years until becoming a warrior. McIntosh hated to leave the training of the young hunter to the older chiefs in the town, but the fighting in the Creek nation demanded his attention. He told Chilly to take care of his sister Jane and baby sister Kate.

As the friendly Creeks formed contingents, General Jackson established Fort Deposit as a supply base at the southernmost point on the Tennessee River. He ordered General John Coffee with the Georgia militia to attack Tallahatche, thirteen miles above Ten Islands, where the Red Sticks made a stand. The rebels were defeated, with 184 dead and 84 taken prisoner. Coffee burned the town, a revenge that Jackson considered appropriate for Fort Mims.

Jackson was plagued by supply shortages, soldiers whose service time was running out, and General John Cocke. Cocke was equal in rank to Jackson and operated independently of him. Jackson had opened negotiations with the Hillabee Indians, who wanted to surrender. While Jackson considered his reply to the Indians, General James White, an officer under Cocke's command, received orders to attack the Hillabee towns. The warriors were waiting for Jackson to accept their surrender, and were totally surprised by the attack. The surviving warriors, confused and angered by this action, resolved to fight the white man to the death.

While Jackson pondered his next move, General Floyd and a thousand Georgia militiamen moved toward Autassee, "Beloved Ground," a town that had been dedicated from ancient times to the sacred art of war. Major McIntosh and Major Barnard were at first tolerated by General Floyd as onlookers rather than welcomed as friendly allies.[11] Floyd launched a surprise attack, catching the Red Sticks in their tents. The Tallisee king, known as "the Great Conjuror," was killed by cannon shot. The Autassee king was also killed in the fury of the battle. After the initial surprise the Red Sticks rallied and waged a fierce battle. Smoke from the rifle fire settled over the battle area like a deadly haze. At one point, when the militiamen were endangered by the rebels, McIntosh and Barnard immediately led their warriors to counter the rebel attack. They responded with such courage and distinction that they were specifically commended by General Floyd in his report of the battle.[12] (There was evidence from the battle that these were the same Red Sticks who had attacked Fort Mims. Tecumseh's magic had not worked after all.)

General Floyd had been wounded in the battle of Autassee, so General Coffee assumed command of the Georgia militia. Major McIntosh, who had won his admiration and confidence, was given freedom to conduct mop-up operations in rebel towns, which he proceeded to do. McIntosh was fast learning army tactics and techniques of warfare, and he was learning to think like an army officer.

General Jackson next marched to Tallapoosa, where his troops defeated about five hundred rebels. "Old Hickory," as he came to be known, then moved to attack the Red Sticks at Enotochocpo. There the rebels fought a do-or-die battle, forcing the troops to retreat to Fort Strother. Mutiny became a serious problem for Jackson. Soldiers' terms of enlistment were ending, and they wanted to go back to their farms. They were tired of fighting what seemed to be an endless war with Indians. They were not adequately dressed for the winters and food was often scarce. It was a most discouraging time. Even so, his friends in Tennessee managed to raise a volunteer force of five thousand men, including friendly Creeks, Cherokees, and Choctaws.

Jackson moved toward Tohopeka, or "Horseshoe Bend," on the Tallapoosa River. The Red Sticks had fortified it with a zigzag log barricade at the neck of the peninsula, a defense that the rebels had learned from the army. The log fence stood six to eight feet high, with portholes for deadly crossfire (similar to the fortifications at Fort Sinquefield). Gathered in the fortified area was the cream of the Red Sticks' fighting force, about one thousand chiefs and warriors drawn from the Upper Towns of Oakfuskee, New Youka, Oakshays, Hillabee, Eufaulu, and Fish Ponds.[13] Monahee, a convert to Tecumseh, was spiritual leader and principal chief. Menawa was the war commander.

The rolling Tallapoosa River offered a 200-foot watery barrier around the peninsula. The Red Sticks had determined to resist Jackson's forces to the end. The warriors and their families had moved into the cabins on the lower end of the peninsula, not far from the river.

On March 24, 1814, General Jackson's army began the arduous task of cutting through a 52½-mile wilderness between the Coosa and Tallapoosa rivers, as late winter's chilly winds blew against the men's faces. Two days later they camped about six miles northwest of Horseshoe Bend. Then, on March 27, at 6:30 A.M., Jackson ordered his troops to break camp and march toward the Red Sticks' fortified position on the bend. He also ordered General Coffee, with his army of Indian warriors, to cross the Tallapoosa north of the river bend. Then they were to move south to a position opposite the bend, surrounding the peninsula. This was both a diversionary tactic and a way of cutting off the Red Sticks' possible retreat across the river.[14] When they arrived, General Coffee lined his Indian forces along the edge of the woods. Captain William Russell's company of Indian "spies" took their positions behind the trees, under the cover of evergreen foliage.

Coffee's line of warriors was composed of friendly Creeks under Major McIntosh and Major Barnard and Cherokees under Colonel Gidean Morgan. Among the Cherokees were Ensign John Ross, George (Sequoyah) Guess and Major Ridge. Sam Houston was an ensign in the U.S. 39th Infantry. Coffee positioned men with rifles near the water's edge to snipe at any escaping rebels, a strategy that resulted in more than two hundred dead Red Sticks. The rifles had an effective range of two hundred feet, the approximate width of the river.

Jackson's troops, the East and Middle Tennessee Infantry, and the Thirty-Ninth Regiment faced the log fence. They fired sporadically at the painted faces that popped up above the logs. The troops were restless, waiting for Jackson's orders to attack. The general had mounted one three-pounder and one six-pounder on a pine knoll about fifty yards to the right of the log barrier. The cannons fired for two hours at the log fence in the cold March air, but to no effect. Jackson's troops began to creep closer to the zigzag barrier.

The friendly Indians, under Coffee, heard the cannon fire and grew eager to cross the river and join the fighting on the peninsula. Some warriors, apparently without orders, jumped into the river and swam to the canoes intended for the rebels' escape. The warriors paddled the canoes back and forth across the river until a force of Indians landed on the peninsula. The warriors, in force, attacked the Red Sticks and burned the village of huts.

This singular action served as a catalyst to the troops waiting impatiently in front of the log fence. Soldiers and militiamen, hearing the shots and yells below and seeing the smoke and flames rising from the lower peninsula, begged Jackson for the signal to attack. The general felt that he could no longer restrain the enthusiasm of the troops and ordered the attack.

The army that surged toward the log barricade was a curious mixture. The regulars, with officers dressed in long-tailed military uniforms and high hats with plumes, moved forward in military line. The militiamen, surged toward the Red Stick defense with frontier abandon. Jackson's force charged the zigzag log barrier with rifles, muskets, and swords. As they drew close to the log barricade, crossfire poured from the portholes, and soldiers in

Jackson's troops attacking the Red Sticks' fortification.

the front line of the attack fell—dead or wounded. Major Lemuel P. Montgomery, for whom the county in Alabama is named, leaped atop the wall and yelled for his men to follow. At that moment, a bullet from the rebels hit him in the head, killing him instantly.

Major McIntosh and Major Barnard had led the friendly Indian forces across the river and now grouped to attack the rebels. McIntosh and Barnard, who were now veterans of battles against the Red Sticks, led their warriors to engage the rebels.

Inside the log fence the Red Sticks' attention was divided between the friendly Indians battling further up the peninsula and the attack of soldiers on the fence. Monahee, the spiritual leader of the rebels, yelled to the warriors to resist the Indians who were fighting up the hill. Menawa, the war leader, yelled for the warriors to remain at the fence and repel the troops. The rebels seemed confused, looking first at Monahee, then Menawa. Finally, the War Chief, in a rage at poor tactics, killed Monahee. Then, ordering the warriors to fight at the fence, he jumped into the battle with complete disregard for his own life.

The battle raged throughout the day as Jackson's troops and rebel Indians exchanged rifle and musket fire, creating a haze on the battleground. Tomahawks struck flesh, arrows swiftly sought their targets, and swords winked in the sun as they harvested human life. As the powder ran out, soldiers and Indians alike swung rifles as weapons and fought in hand-to-hand combat. Often they stumbled over the bodies that now littered the field.

Ensign Sam Houston, twenty-one years old, was hit in the thigh by an arrow. Later he received two shoulder wounds, from which he nearly died. Menawa fought with incredible strength, though suffering from seven bullet wounds and several stab wounds. He finally dropped and was left for dead. When he came to, he slowly raised himself on one elbow. He noted that the soldiers who were prodding the bodies of warriors to see whether they were still alive were passing over dead Indian women sprawled on the battlefield. Two dead women were about fifteen feet away. He crawled cautiously over to them, stripped the blood-soaked dress off one, pulled it on himself,[15] then passed out.

A soldier came by just as Menawa regained consciousness, and he instinctively grabbed for the soldier's leg. The weary fighter swung his rifle toward Menawa's head but fired too quickly. The shot tore away part of Menawa's face and several teeth. The shot stunned Menawa and the soldier thought he was dead. After darkness fell, the half-dead Menawa crawled down to the banks of the river, found a canoe, and escaped.

The fighting stopped at dusk. Major McIntosh and his warriors, weary from the long day of battle, tended their wounded and dead. Long out of gunpowder and lead, they cleaned their knives and tomahawks.

The next morning troops and friendly Indians found and killed rebel survivors hidden in the thick brush, bringing the battle of Horseshoe Bend to a close.

The victorious General Jackson, in an unusual move, was offered a commission as a brigadier general in the United States Army. Four days later he was promoted to major general. On August 9, 1814, at old Fort Toulouse (later renamed Fort Jackson), Jackson negotiated a treaty, not with the defeated Red Sticks, but with the friendly Indians. He acted as sole negotiator, permitting neither Agent Hawkins nor the United States commissioners (who were authorized by the federal government to work out the treaty) to determine boundaries.

The general proceeded to demand an L-shaped portion of land, falling mostly in the territory of the Creek Lower Towns. The indemnity was twenty million acres of land,[16] extending across the southern portion of what is today the state of Alabama, across the Chattahoochee eastward to a point on the Georgia coast. The territory extended from the Cherokee boundary (in north Georgia) south to the Florida line. The land lay roughly between the Coosa and the Tombigbee rivers, separating the Creeks from all her Indian neighbors, except the Cherokees and the Spanish.

Jackson's terms for peace did not even distinguish the Red Sticks from the friendly Creeks. Big Warrior, who had not rebelled, argued that the terms were unreasonable, that they took too much land from the Lower Towns. Major McIntosh, Major Barnard, and

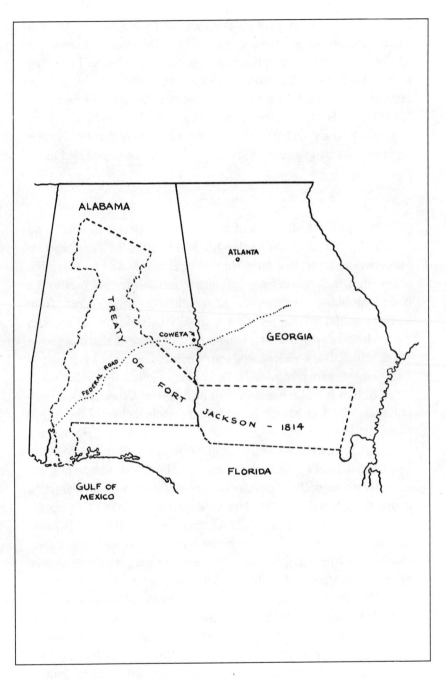

The area of land demanded by Jackson.

Noble Kinnard argued strongly that they had fought hard for Jackson against the rebels. Jackson, however, gave the chiefs no credit for bravery, only for presumption and ignorance, and he badly wanted to end the threat of the rebel Creeks. None of the Red Sticks were present, so he made an unusual and extreme demand to accomplish his purpose: He forced the friendly Creeks, who fought with him, to sign the treaty that the rebel chiefs should have signed. Further argument seemed useless. Agent Hawkins, disgusted, offered to resign.

· · ·

Major McIntosh's term of active military service had ended on March 27, just after the battle. All Indian allies of Jackson were mustered out of service after Horseshoe Bend. McIntosh won high praise and, in fact, was singled out by Jackson for his part in the battle. McIntosh's experience as a field commander grew from battle to battle, and his warriors gradually moved from hit-and-run skirmish tactics to the stand-and-fight boldness of the Horseshoe Bend battle. The Creek chiefs and warriors now held McIntosh in high respect, partly because he had chosen the winning side.

McIntosh had become a central figure in Creek military and political influence, having been elected principal chief of the Lower Creeks.[17] His new affluence included two new wives. He married Susannah Roe, a Cherokee. A daughter, Rebecca, was born to them. His third wife, Peggy, also a Cherokee, bore him three children.

McIntosh built a large, two-story home on a small plantation above the Chattahoochee. Here he enjoyed the style of living for which he had worked so hard. Another Creek chief, Big Warrior, was equally as wealthy. In contrast were the hut or small cabin-dwellings of the majority of the Creek Indians, which were adequate, but not as comfortable or spacious.

The months of peace following the battle of Horseshoe Bend allowed the major to cultivate the flat land beside the river, to grow corn and raise cattle and hogs. He kept his seventy-two Negro slaves busy tending crops and caring for the livestock. Chilly and Jane were sent to Milledgeville Academy to learn English and the culture of the whites. McIntosh had seen the advantages of living in both cultures and wanted to give his children the best of both worlds.

His wives Peggy and Susannah both had wardrobes reflecting post-Colonial styles fashionable at the time. They wore silk and cotton dresses, cloaks, and gowns. Their wardrobes included cashmere, silk, and cotton shawls, and gold and silver earrings. In the home were books on travel, geography, and the English language. For entertainment they read *Gulliver's Travels* and *Robinson Crusoe*.

Chief McIntosh and Chilly had frontier gentlemen's wardrobes. They owned pistols and holsters, boots, spurs, and rifles. For the plantation they had purchased a variety of farming tools, hogs, cattle, and horses. To maintain his plantation, McIntosh kept several thousand dollars in cash at his home, profits from his business enterprises.[18]

The effect of the Red Sticks' war on the Creek Nation was disastrous. The Creeks were broken and dispirited. Creek women labored hard for food, and warriors often drank too much whiskey. Most signs of resistance had gone, and General Jackson boasted that he had broken the power of the Creeks forever.[19] Menawa's nearly fatal wounds took a year to heal, after which he resumed leadership of the Hillabee towns. Peter McQueen, the Red Ground chief, Joseph Francis, and other Red Stick leaders retreated to the Florida Everglades and joined the Seminoles.

The Red Sticks' defiance was not over. Admiral Alexander Cochrane, senior British officer in North America, received permission from the Spanish to land a combat-training party at Mobile. This was part of the British effort during the War of 1812. Major Edward Nicholls and Captain Woodbine, along with 8 other officers and 130 soldiers, composed the combat-training party. They recruited Red Sticks and runaway Negro slaves for combat. The slaves, 300 in number, were equipped as the Black Marine Battalion to raid southern towns. A number of Upper Town chiefs were in Cochrane's pay, as was Bowlegs, a chief of the Seminoles. Cochrane also hired interpreters among the Red Sticks, such as George, Daniel, and Samuel Perryman, Alexander Durant, and John Baptiste. Of special note was Lieutenant William Hamby, "Head Interpreter of the Creek Nation."[20] Hamby was also an interpreter for the

U.S. Government, which raises the possibility that he was a double-agent, although nothing about his activity would indicate this.

McIntosh was angry at Jackson's unreasonable treaty demands and had voiced his disapproval. He, like other Creek officers, now faced a harsh reality: they could not rebel against the growing might of the U. S. Army and win.

Big Warrior, disgusted with Jackson's unreasonable treaty demands, seems to have leaned toward British influence at Mobile. Nevertheless, he asked Major McIntosh to carry word to Agent Hawkins, not to Jackson, that the British were using Pensacola to arm runaway Negro slaves. General Jackson had already written to McIntosh to raise a force of Creeks and move against the British establishment at Apalachicola. Receiving word about the Black Battalion, McIntosh diverted his warriors toward Pensacola and attacked the Negroes with five hundred braves. During the fighting, one hundred Negroes were killed, and the remaining two hundred were returned to their masters.

Major McIntosh, observing that the fort at Apalachicola could be taken, wrote a note to that effect to Jackson. The secretary of war gave his approval for an attack. The fort was manned by a mixture of runaway slaves, Seminoles, and rebel Creeks who had fled to Florida after the defeat at Horseshoe Bend. This motley group of malcontents had been raiding southern Georgia towns. The Red Sticks' resistance was down but not out. A mop-up operation seemed desirable.

Major McIntosh and two hundred warriors moved to attack the fort at Apalachicola. At the same time Colonel Duncan Clinch was ordered to attack the British-supported fort. In July 1816 the combined forces of army troops and friendly Creeks attacked the town. The battle was cut short, however, when a cannonball made a direct hit on a well-stocked ammunition magazine inside the fort. The resulting explosion blew the fort apart, killing the people inside.

Red Sticks and Seminoles continued to maraud southern Georgia territory, so Secretary of War John C. Calhoun ordered Jackson to attack these rebels.

About 1817 William McIntosh was promoted to brigadier general, in command of a brigade of more than thirteen hundred Creek warriors.[21] The nineteen company commanders included his half brother, Captain Roley McIntosh, Captain William Miller, Mad Wolf, and son-in-law Samuel Hawkins (Samuel had married McIntosh's daughter Jane). One of these companies came from Au-muc-cul-le, where Jackson's troops replenished their supplies.

Jackson ordered General McIntosh and his brigade to Fort Gadsden, which had been built on the old site at Apalachicola. On the way McIntosh's warriors ran into some Red Sticks, and fighting broke out. McIntosh notified Jackson that he had captured three rebels and was bringing them to Fort Gadsden. He also added that he expected to catch more of the marauding Red Sticks before reaching the fort. When the brigade arrived, McIntosh dealt with the captives according to Indian law—he executed them.

General McIntosh heard that the Red Ground chief, who had escaped from Horseshoe Bend, had gathered a number of rebels about forty miles below Fort Gaines and was threatening the southern area of Georgia with raids. McIntosh's brigade moved on March 10, 1817, through the blustery chill to round up the Red Sticks and reported to Jackson that he had captured fourteen of them. The women and children of the Red Sticks were sent back to Eufaulu. Later, ten more rebels surrendered. The fighting continued into the next day, when McIntosh hoped to capture the Red Ground chief. It took three weeks, however, to capture the leaders, including the chief, and win the skirmish. McIntosh's brigade then joined General Jackson at St. Mary's, about sixty miles from the Apalachicola River.

General McIntosh and his brigade proceeded, on orders from Jackson, toward Suwanee on April 1. The warriors marched past fresh spring buds waving in the breeze. Their eyes searched the woods, beyond the spring flowers, for the faces of Red Sticks. Suwanee was the town of Chief Boleck or "Bowlegs," where they would begin a strategic corralling of the remaining rebels. While marching from St. Mary's toward Suwanee on April 12, McIntosh received word that Pete McQueen, a rebel chief, was in the area. The regular army remained on the road, as was its custom, while the warriors of the brigade went to search the woods for Red Sticks. They encountered the rebels near a swampy area, and fighting broke out, lasting for about an hour. Arrows and guns hit more trees than flesh in the densely wooded area. The Red Sticks waded as quickly as they could through the swamp in a retreat from the overwhelming numbers of the brigade. The rebels found cover and stopped in an area full of thickets, from which they had visual advantage over the oncoming warriors. Fire erupted from the unseen rebels. The brigade warriors, frustrated by an invisible enemy, fired in the direction of the shots and at movements in the brush. Crouching warriors advanced from tree to tree, trying to spot the rebels.

Smoke from rifles and muskets began to fill the woods like an afternoon fog. Several friendly Creeks fell as they caught enemy fire. Red Sticks fell, wounded or dead, by clumps of bushes. War cries from both sides of the fighting filled the woods as rebels and brigade warriors fought in hand-to-hand combat. Bravery was not lacking on either side, but skills that had developed in earlier skirmishes and battles tipped the scales in favor of the seasoned warriors. Heavy fighting continued for several hours.

Suddenly, the shrieks of women's voices could be heard above the din of battle. One voice was that of a woman speaking English. General McIntosh immediately ordered Major Tom Woodward, Captain Isaac Brown, and Billy Mitchell forward to free the women. The women were huddled in a thicket of cabbage trees, caught between the fire of the combatants. Brown rushed in, killing a Red Stick who challenged his advance. Woodward took aim at a rebel near the women, but a shot blasted his rifle in two just behind the lock. He grasped a musket handed to him by a soldier and continued to fire. Mitchell, a good soldier, but crippled by arthritis, did not reach the women as quickly as did Brown and Woodward. Creek and Uchee warriors joined in freeing the three women and several children from their Red Stick captivity.

The white woman whom they had heard speaking English was Mrs. Stewart. She had been captured earlier when rebels had attacked an army supply boat that she and her husband, a sergeant, had been aboard. All on board, except Mrs. Stewart and two soldiers, had been killed by the raiders. Her presence among the Red Sticks was a complete surprise to McIntosh's warriors.

The brigade pressed the fighting for about two more hours

while the remaining Red Sticks retreated into the woods. When the battle was over, the friendly Creeks had lost three dead, five wounded. The Red Sticks lost thirty-seven dead from about two hundred warriors from five Upper Town areas.[22] The brigade also confiscated many head of cattle, hogs, and quantities of corn.

General McIntosh's leadership during the battle won awe and respect from his junior officers. The general's own feelings about the battle are reflected in a letter to Agent D. B. Mitchell:

> Tom Woodward and Mr. Brown, and your son our agent, and all the white men in our country were with us through the whole fight, and fought well. All my officers fought so well I do not know which is the bravest. They all fought well and ran the enemies.[23]

· · ·

By the end of April 1819 most of the troublesome element of the Red Sticks had been killed or captured in Florida. The prophet Francis was hanged. The elusive Peter McQueen and Hossa Yoholo, their followers starving and dying of disease, were hiding among the Seminoles in the Everglades. With few exceptions, such as Menawa, none of the rebellious chiefs of the Creek nation were now in power.

By April 24, 1819, General McIntosh and his brigade were mustered out of service. Now in his mid-forties, McIntosh had spent six years fighting the Red Sticks and their allies.

On reaching Coweta, he was told of the bizarre killing of his uncle, Chief Howard, at Au-muc-cul-le, one of the Chechehaw villages of the Indian Confederacy. While McIntosh and his warriors had been in Florida fighting the Red Sticks and the Seminoles, two chiefs of the Chechehaw tribe—Hopawnee and Philemme—had taken part in raids on the southern Georgia frontier. Georgia Governor William Rabun ordered Jackson to send troops to destroy the Indian towns, but the general, engaged in skirmishes and pursuit of the Red Sticks, ignored the order. Angered by the disobedience, Rabun ordered Captain Obed Wright of the Georgia militia to carry out the order.

Captain Wright marched his troops toward the Chechehaw towns and received reports that warriors from Au-muc-cul-le had taken part in the raids. When he reached Fort Early, near the village, Wright received information from Captain Bothwell, the fort commander, that the Chechehaw villages were friendly toward the government. Wright refused to accept the information, and the next day his troops attacked Au-muc-cul-le. As the fighting intensified, some warriors escaped into the swamp. Troops set fire to houses, sometimes with women and children inside. Aging Chief Howard, an uncle of General McIntosh, emerged, waving a white flag of surrender. Another Indian came out, carrying a baby in his arms. Both were killed instantly by the troops. Chief Howard's earrings were torn from his ears and worn by the adjutant of the troops.

McIntosh demanded of General Jackson that Wright be punished and that a letter of apology be sent to the Chechehaw warriors in his command. Jackson responded by having Wright arrested and brought to his headquarters. Governor Rabun, however, challenged Jackson's authority to arrest the captain. Heated correspondence was exchanged, but Wright was finally released without punishment.

Menawa hated General McIntosh's popularity and influence. The badly scarred veteran of Horseshoe Bend returned to the Creek Nation as one of its leaders. He had soured on the American government in general and McIntosh in particular. Big Warrior, who often acted as principal chief, along with Little Prince, was suspicious of McIntosh's popularity. Other chiefs had taken note of his suspicion as early as at the treaty of Fort Toulouse.[24] This suspicion would continue to grow, in spite of McIntosh's repeated efforts to help his people deal with the inevitable encroachment of the U. S. government.

III

Georgia's Push for the Removal of All Indians

GEORGIANS were growing more impatient for the removal of all Indians from their land, as agreed to in the treaty of 1805. At the time of the treaty, the new federal government was perhaps not sure of its strength to effect a removal, but Jackson's victory at Horseshoe Bend was a profound military shot in the arm to the growing might of the United States.

The Creeks, defeated and broken, were painfully aware of their shrinking lands and determined to hold fast the remaining territory. The Indian refugees returned from the war to rebuild their ravaged towns. Game for food was low, and community agriculture was nearly gone. Creek women were being forced into more labor, and drunkenness among the warriors was becoming a serious problem. Most Creeks could not return to their old way of life: it had disappeared, and they had not learned another.[1]

Earlier, before the war, McIntosh is said to have proposed the revolutionary idea of Creeks' adopting much of the American culture (seen especially in his favoring the Christian missions) in order to save the Indian culture from near-extinction.[2] The devastated Creek economy was now heavily dependent on the white man. Tribal chiefs of the Lower Towns, having had early contact with the Americans, tended to be more easily persuaded by United States Indian agents, such as the late Benjamin Hawkins and his successor, David Bridie Mitchell. An agent's word carried heavy political and military weight. Mitchell was a successful politician in Georgia, having served as its governor from 1815 to 1817. Tiring of the political arena, however, he asked, with blatantly self-serving motives, to be named Indian agent.[3] Part of the Indian agent's responsibility was to appoint an Indian to sell goods within the Indian nations. The appointed merchant was then expected to give to the government agent a percentage of the profits from these sales, which amount would probably exceed the governor's salary. No doubt Mitchell found this arrangement appealing.

The outcome of the Red Sticks' war polarized the Upper and the Lower Towns more than ever. Little Prince, the venerated ninety-year-old wise man, was principal chief. Next was Big Warrior, chief of the Upper Towns and their speaker. William McIntosh, now forty-three years old, was ranked fifth in the Creek Nation, but his influence probably exceeded his rank. He was now speaker of the National Council, a position of high honor, for he spoke the thoughts of the principal chief in tribal councils. He also remained head chief of the Lower Towns.

Little Prince, Big Warrior, McIntosh, and other chiefs had been on the Red Sticks' "hit list" but had survived the marauders' attacks. Big Warrior's jealousy of McIntosh, however, was more than the passing agitation he had felt at the treaty at Fort Jackson. Further, there is little question that Menawa, badly scarred from near-fatal wounds received at the battle of Horseshoe Bend, had helped to stir resentment against McIntosh.

Another result of the war was the removal of the Creek national capital from Tuckabatchee to Broken Arrow (Thleancotehean), near the west bank of the Chattahoochee, about six miles below present-day Columbus, Georgia.[4] This moving of the capital may have been due to the attack by the Red Sticks.

General Jackson and his troops had just returned from the swampy pockets of Florida where they had fought the remnants of the rebelling Creeks and the hostile Seminoles. Chief McIntosh returned to the nation and disbanded his brigade, having won more military honors than he had at the battle of Horseshoe Bend.

Hardly had the dust settled on the Florida campaign when President James Monroe commissioned Indian Agent David B. Mitchell to negotiate with the defeated and dispirited Creek nation. The Creeks, having earlier yielded to the friendly persuasion of

General Oglethorpe, had, by 1763, ceded to the British colonists all lands facing the Atlantic Ocean. Creeks and Cherokees had ceded all the frontier border between Georgia and South Carolina by 1790. By the treaty of 1804 the Creeks ceded about one-third of what is now the state of Georgia.

Agent Mitchell asked Big Warrior, Little Prince, William McIntosh, and fifteen other chiefs of the Creek Nation to meet at the Creek agency on the Flint River on January 23, 1818. This treaty did not follow a military defeat, as did the one at Fort Jackson, so the mood was businesslike and moderately friendly. The ceded territory lay in two parts: the first part, roughly the land along the Ocmulgee River (by Macon) and along the Oconee River (near Dublin), down to the confluence with the Altamaha River (about twenty miles south of Uvalda), and along the St. Mary's River in southeast Georgia, along the Florida border; the other part lay between the Appalachee River (by the Georgia towns of Auburn and Appalachee) and the Chattahoochee River.[5]

Americans, ever eager to push the frontier westward, were quickly settling newly ceded territory, and inevitably, the laws of both cultures were broken. The United States brought its laws to bear on frontiersmen and Indians alike. The Creeks decided to discard old tribal laws, which had been carried by oral tradition, and to write new ones to encourage harmony between Indians and whites. Chief McIntosh's knowledge of the minds and the languages of both cultures and his ability to write English came into play. He wrote the Creek laws in 1817; other laws adopted by the council that year, to deal with encroaching whites and retaliating Creeks, were a combination of Creek and federal laws. There was, however, no equality of justice in the application of the laws. Creeks who murdered whites were immediately hunted down and executed. Whites who murdered Indians, however, seldom received such punishment.

McIntosh sent a letter to Agent D. B. Mitchell, expressing his hope:

> These are the laws I have made for my Nation, and have given up our old laws that our old people had in their old ways. I hope they will raise our Nation, and make all our

poor people love one another, and love our white brothers. And we have considered that we will make it the law to love all other friendly Indians, as we wish to be friendly to all, as I am friendly to the United States of America. My head warriors have agreed to these laws, and have signed them with us, and I hope you our agent will also agree to them.

Mitchell modified only two of fifty-seven laws.[6]

Even with laws written to help protect both cultures, Georgians remained fearful of the Indians and now pressed the government to move the Creeks west of the Mississippi River. Chief McIntosh and other tribal leaders continued to consider moving to the West, but this idea had not gained favor with most chiefs.[7] To encourage better understanding, the chief continued to introduce headmen to the American culture and Americans to the Indians. He took a group of Creeks to worship at the Methodist church in Milledgeville, Georgia, then visited the governor later. The townspeople were impressed with the orderly conduct of the Indians, and they made note of McIntosh's polished manners and intelligence. On dress occasions he wore his chief's turban with a long feather and his red-trimmed cape spread over broad shoulders. His shirt of Scottish plaid was tucked into Indian-style buckskin trousers. Over his left shoulder hung the sacred sash of a Creek chief, its brightly colored beads woven meticulously into a zigzag pattern. On official occasions he added an elaborate army officer's sword given to him by the state of Georgia.

Between military engagements and after the war McIntosh divided his time among his three wives, raising families with each. The chief's first son, Chilly, by his first wife, Eliza, was now eighteen. His skin was light enough to pass for white, though his high cheekbones reflected his Indian heritage. Had the brigade not mustered out when it did, Chilly would probably have joined his father's warriors in the Florida campaign. Jane had married Billy Mitchell, son of the agent. This union did not last, and Jane then married Samuel Hawkins, of the Creek Nation. A colonel in McIntosh's brigade, he was now a secretary to the chief. Kate, the youngest

On dress occasions Chief William McIntosh wore the sash of a Creek chief over his shirt of Scottish plaid.

daughter of Chief William and Eliza, was probably in her early teens. Negro slaves tended the livestock and farmed the plantation where Eliza and the family lived. By his second wife, Susannah, the chief now had a three-year-old named Rebecca, who freely roamed the woods around Acorn Bluff, investigating all parts of the plantation by the Chattahoochee. Her primary interest, however, was in her new sister, Delilah. Also at Acorn Bluff lived Peggy, the chief's third wife, by whom he probably now had a child. All indications point to a harmonious relationship between Peggy and Susannah.

Chilly McIntosh built a home near Broken Arrow and went into business with his father, establishing a trading post at Fort Mitchell. They used an abandoned store and factory, and hired George Stinson, the chief's brother-in-law, to run it. Agent Mitchell, who was probably in partnership with the McIntoshes, is likely to have encouraged Stinson to go into the Creek Nation to sell goods. Indians could buy at the trading post with annuity funds or on credit. McIntosh demanded that Indians who traded at the post spend all of their annuities there, a practice that the warriors disliked.

Mitchell was later charged with misappropriation of Creek indemnities and smuggling slaves across the line into Georgia. For those offenses he was dismissed as agent, although there is reason to believe that the accusations were trumped up.

Chief McIntosh's business enterprises grew; he had an instinct for trade that was shrewd and aggressive. He ran the ferry (known as the "McIntosh Ferry") from Coweta across the Chattahoochee River. Between 1818 and 1823 he and a relative, Joe Baillie, built a tavern-inn, located at present-day Indian Springs, Georgia. The inn was built near the mineral springs, which enjoyed a wide reputation for healing powers.

It was an impressive structure with large rooms, rising two stories and with a long porch facing the well-worn trail that brought tired travelers to its doors. Chimneys were built at both ends of the long roof, over fireplaces whose roaring fires heated the rooms during the long winter nights.

On the walls were etchings, *Courageous Timoclea Before Alexander the Great, The Warrior and the Chief, Death of Napoleon,*

The McIntosh tavern-inn.

and *The Battle of Missiloughi,* which reflected McIntosh's interest in battles, chiefs, and leaders.[8] A piano in the dining room was probably used to entertain dinner guests. Lodging was $1.25 per day, dinner 50¢, and breakfast and supper were 37½¢ each. Meals were served punctually: breakfast at 8 A.M., dinner at 2 P.M., and evening tea at 7 P.M. A bell rang ten minutes before each meal to allow the ladies to be seated first at the table. No drunks were allowed in the inn, and the doors were closed every night at 11 P.M.

Provisions were made for servants and travelers' horses. During one season eight hundred weary travelers enjoyed the comforts of the wilderness lodge. The inn met the food and shelter needs of the growing number of wayfarers who traveled the newly opened lands of the Indians.

Government leaders, chiefs and headmen of Indian nations, and travelers came to Acorn Bluff in such numbers that McIntosh built, close to his home on the knoll, a cabin furnished with beds. He was now one of the wealthiest Indians of the Creek Nation. Both he and Big Warrior owned land, livestock, and Negro slaves.

The tension over leadership between the two chiefs grew as McIntosh assumed a stronger role in the nation and at councils. He had been the victor in the fight against the Red Sticks; Big Warrior, an experienced warrior-chief and pro-American, had never left Tuckabatchee to fight the Red Sticks. McIntosh, a general, wielded influence and power that approached Big Warrior's own in the nation. This tension became apparent when land ceded in the treaty at Fort Jackson was to be surveyed.

This treaty called for a line between the Creek and the Cherokee nations in what is now northern Georgia. The surveyors began their work in 1821 under the watchful eye of Dick Brown, representing the Cherokees, and Chief McIntosh and Big Warrior, representing the Creeks. Hardly had the surveyor begun when Brown objected to the placement of the line, saying that it was too far north and into Cherokee territory. McIntosh responded that the land being surveyed was part of a concession of land made by the Creeks to the Cherokees, who had lost much in fighting the Americans.[9] Finally, the leaders agreed to fix the boundary on the east side of the Coosa River, down to a point below Tuckabatchee, then southeast to the Chattahoochee River.

As the surveyor's chain was pulled across the ground, Big Warrior began to protest the losing of the tribal lands and declared that the line should not be extended eastward. Lower Creek warriors joined in the protest, but little could be done in the presence of the eight hundred federal soldiers stationed at Fort Mitchell.

Then, on March 17, 1820, President James Monroe presented to the United States Senate a request for money to extinguish all Indian ownership of lands in the state of Georgia.[10] It was noted that the Cherokees and the Creeks had taken property of considerable value from the citizens of Georgia and that treaties made so far had not recovered the land. This claim—that Indians had taken Georgia land—was an absolute fabrication. Georgia demanded that the federal government honor the agreement contained in the treaty of 1802, a stipulation calling for the cession of the west bank of the Chattahoochee River north to Uchee Creek and extending north to the Cherokee village of Nickajack on the Tennessee River. The Americans wanted cession of a corridor that would run eastward to Alabama and north between the Creeks and the Cherokees, separating the tribes.

The United States commissioners in charge of Indian affairs met in 1821 with Little Prince, McIntosh, and other chiefs, at McIntosh's inn at Indian Springs to sign a treaty. The commissioners shocked the assembled chiefs with charges that Georgia had claims against the Creek Nation (dating back to the Revolutionary War) and demands for a half-million dollars. The claim was fraudulent. McIntosh, speaking for the Creeks, strongly protested the claim but was pressured to recognize the debt. It is likely that the chief felt that counterdemands and debate were useless. The Creeks could only hope to cede their land for as much money as they could get. The earlier inclinations to resist forced removal, which McIntosh had once felt and proclaimed, were mellowing into a survival stance—a hope for a better land and a better life beyond the Mississippi. Later that year, at the Creek National Council, Little Prince and McIntosh were censured for having signed the treaty. Both claimed that it had been done to pay a large debt owed to the United States. The council then accepted the treaty.[11]

The treaty won not only the northern corridor but Georgia's entire western boundary from the Ocmulgee to the Flint River, five million acres. The Creeks were initially to receive $50,000, followed by annual payments totalling $150,000 over a fourteen-year period. It was further stipulated that part of this money would be paid by the Creeks to satisfy Georgia's depredation claims. The commissioners agreed to set aside a one-thousand-acre reservation for Chief McIntosh at Indian Springs and a plot of land one mile square on the west bank of the Ocmulgee, at the site of old Fort Hawkins. This gave rise to allegations that McIntosh was a lackey of the Americans and increased Big Warrior's antagonism toward both McIntosh and the Americans.

The tension grew between the Creeks and the U. S. government over the demands to cede land. The Creeks had, by succeeding treaties, ceded over half of their land. They desperately held on to the remaining woods, lakes, and rivers. The whites, however, persisted in their demands for more land. Though Upper Towns chiefs remained adamant, there was probably an unspoken acknowledgment that the U. S. Army held military superiority. Not to enter into a treaty eventually meant loss of life or land. Both Menawa and Opothle Yoholo, veterans of the War of 1812, knew this. Still, instinctively, they held on to their beloved land.

The urgency with which Georgia pursued the removal of all Indians from the land rose to a fever pitch when George M. Troup was appointed governor in 1823. He was a feisty politician who realized that his power came from the people who had voted for his appointment and whom he passionately sought to please. Further, Troup was a first cousin of Chief McIntosh; Troup's mother was Catherine McIntosh, a sister of William, the chief's father. There is no indication that the men were close; their correspondence is businesslike, demonstrating no strong feelings of kinship. Troup corresponded vigorously with President Monroe for the removal of all Indians from Georgia. He also urged Chief McIntosh to use his influence to persuade the Creeks to cede their lands in the state.

When Chief McIntosh's friend and (probably) business partner, D. B. Mitchell, was dismissed as Indian agent, John Crowell was assigned to the office. Crowell, who had been Alabama's first congressional delegate, plunged into Georgia politics and openly sided with gubernatorial candidate John Clark and the anti-Troup party. In his position as Indian agent, he forbade McIntosh to continue distributing annuities to the Creeks. The chief, instead of giving credit or change from the full amount of an Indian's annuity, made him spend the full amount on merchandise from the trading post, a practice that the Creeks did not like. When Crowell took over the distribution of annuities, however, he paid the Indians only in large bills, fifties and one-hundreds. The Indians, again, had to buy more merchandise than they needed.

The agent's brother, Thomas Crowell, had opened a trading post in competition with McIntosh, and the chief responded by lowering his prices and outselling Crowell. John Crowell, as the Indian agent, disbursed the annuities, or money owed the Indians by treaty with the U. S. government. When he retaliated by refusing to pay McIntosh for debts incurred by Indians, the Chief went among the debtors in the public square, forcibly taking the money from them. In retaliation, Crowell ordered Stinson's arrest for trading in the Creek Nation without a license. He then took the goods from McIntosh's trading post and gave them to his brother, Thomas. While McIntosh refused to allow Crowell's men to take Stinson into custody, Chilly McIntosh took a force of warriors and seized the confiscated goods.

Crowell was so outdone that he wrote letters to Big Warrior and Little Prince, demanding that McIntosh be "broken" as chief, but the chiefs supported McIntosh. Stinson was tried and acquitted in a federal court in Savannah.

Big Warrior found his conflict with McIntosh aggravated by the resentment of the Indians whose relatives (Red Sticks) had been killed by McIntosh's troops. Crowell's bitterness toward McIntosh made Crowell an ally of sorts of the chiefs of the Upper Towns, who were suspicious of the general. Chief McIntosh saw clearly the complicity in these attitudes and feelings, and the danger they represented for him.

Crowell resisted McIntosh's efforts to teach the Indians Christianity by bringing Methodist and Baptist missionaries to locate near Coweta.[12] It was part of McIntosh's plan to strengthen the Creeks by encouraging them to learn the white man's ways, but Crowell encouraged Big Warrior to resist. The Reverend William Capers, a

Methodist missionary, sent a letter to Secretary of War John C. Calhoun, complaining of Crowell's profanity and frequent appearances at cockfights while neglecting his duties. Calhoun asked Crowell to modify his position and allow the missionaries to continue their work.

While Chief McIntosh sought to strengthen the Creek culture by exposing them to the white man's ways, Governor Troup worked just as hard to remove all Indians from Georgia. His primary administrative goal was the removal of all Creeks and Cherokees. He wrote an urgent appeal to President James Monroe to act on the U. S. government's twenty-year-old promise to remove the Indians from the state of Georgia. In response the president directed United States Commissioners Meriwether and Campbell to go to the Cherokee capital, New Echota, in July 1823, to negotiate with the National Council for land. The Cherokees had earlier sent an immigration party west of the Mississippi, but reports of hardships came back, and there was no interest in selling their Georgia land.

Chief McIntosh, perhaps at the urging of the commissioners, appealed to John Ross, a white man with Indian blood who was president of the Cherokee National Committee and a tribal chief:

1823
Newtown, 21 October

> My friend; I am going to inform you in a few lines as a friend. I want you to give me your opinion about the treaty; whether the chiefs will be willing or not. If the chiefs feel disposed to let the United States have land, [or] part of it. I want you to let me know; I will make the United States Commissioners give you two thousand dollars, A. McCoy the same, and Charles Hicks three thousand dollars, for present, and nobody shall know it; and if you think the land [would not] be sold, I will be satisfied. If the land should be sold, I will get you the amount before the treaty sign; and if you get any friend you want him to receive, they shall receive. Nothing more to inform you at present.
>
> I remain your affectionate friend,
> William McIntosh[13]

The chief intended, of course, that Ross read the letter privately. The Cherokee chief had been a comrade-in-arms at the battle of Horseshoe Bend and an esteemed veteran of skirmishes against the Red Sticks. McIntosh may have reasoned that the Cherokees, like the Creeks, would sooner or later lose their lands to the whites: Why not gain whatever financial advantage they could in the cession? Whatever his thoughts, McIntosh was not ready for Ross's reaction. Three days later the president read the letter aloud in council, in McIntosh's presence. The Cherokee chiefs who listened to the reading were soon in an uproar. Major Ridge, veteran of Horseshoe Bend and a strong admirer of the Creek chief, shouted that McIntosh had forfeited his great honor and his name. The general hastily withdrew from the council and headed home, reflecting on his serious miscalculation of the interests of the Cherokee chiefs. The council voted to exclude McIntosh from Cherokee councils and lands forever.[14]

The commissioners left the council red-faced. The Cherokees sent a runner to Little Prince and Big Warrior, telling them what had happened. They said that they had lost confidence in McIntosh's fidelity to the interests of his red brothers, and they advised a close watch on him, lest he ruin the nation.

McIntosh's activities in the Cherokee council further inflamed Big Warrior's resentment against him, and Big Warrior was determined to stop the chief from selling any more land. The Tuckabatchee chief, apparently with the approval of Little Prince, called for a meeting of the chiefs of the Upper Towns (Alabama) in Tuckabatchee in May 1824. Big Warrior's undeclared agenda was clearly to reduce the influence and power of Chief McIntosh. Agent Crowell was present but, curiously, made no report to the United States commissioners. Nevertheless, he was hardly neutral concerning Big Warrior's feelings toward McIntosh. He may have encouraged the Creeks not to negotiate for any more land. Big Warrior's son-in-law, Captain William Walker, who was sub-agent, wrote the text of the meeting.

By having the gathering in the old capital of the Creek Nation—his seat of power—Big Warrior played strongly on feelings about the former Creek Confederacy's power and influence. The nation's past victories were extolled. The disastrous Red Stick war was remembered and blamed on "crazy young men" who had fought against the United States, an action that had led to treaties and land cessions. The chiefs then resolved that they could survive by developing agriculture and becoming "civilized." They would learn the white man's farming techniques but keep their Indian culture. In this way, they reasoned, they could stay on the land that was left. They resolved to follow the "pattern of the Cherokees," that is, not to sell or trade any more land.[15] The agreement was signed by Big Warrior, Little Prince, and twelve leading chiefs of the Upper Towns. By tradition, only those who signed were bound by the agreement.

One month later, Agent Crowell, on orders from Washington, called for all chiefs to meet the United States commissioners at Broken Arrow to cede more land. While these preparations were underway, the chiefs of the Upper Towns, led by Big Warrior and Little Prince, met at Pole Cat Springs in Alabama, fifty miles west of Broken Arrow. Among those present were Etomme Tustennuggee, a chief of Coweta and a lifelong friend of McIntosh. Also in attendance was the outstanding young Indian orator, Opothle Yoholo. Little Prince, an admirer and supporter of the chief, was stunned by his action in the Cherokee council and now sided with Big Warrior and the chiefs of the Upper Towns in resolving to hold all remaining land. They reenacted the law proclaiming death to any chief who ceded land. Big Warrior orchestrated the meeting so that feelings ran against Chief McIntosh's aborted effort to get the Cherokee chiefs to sell land. The Tuckabatchee chief cut into the general's support by finagling Chief Etommee Tustennuggee's presence at the council and his assent in signing the agreements.[16]

The proceedings were again recorded by Sub-agent Walker and held in his house. He arranged for the writings to be published in the Alabama newspapers. Big Warrior used both meetings, at Tuckabatchee and Pole Cat Springs, to scare the chiefs and warriors of the Lower Towns who were followers of McIntosh, a strategy that proved most effective.

Commissioners Duncan Campbell and James Meriwether first heard of the councils on their way to the meetings at Broken Arrow.[17] Chief McIntosh, who had gone to his home at Indian Springs, was given newspaper accounts of those meetings. He vehemently denied the validity of any law except those passed in public council at Broken Arrow. A little later, before the meeting at Broken Arrow, McIntosh seems to have wavered from his resolve that the Creek Nation should cede its eastern lands and move west of the Mississippi, for he told a public meeting of Indians of the Lower Towns at a ball game that anyone who sold land would forfeit his life. This change of attitude was temporary, however, for he later talked with the chiefs and the headmen to convince them that a treaty should be worked out to cede the rest of the Creek lands in Georgia.

Although his influence among his people had been strained by the Cherokee fiasco, the chief still wielded considerable influence among the Lower Creek Indians. Memories were not so short that tribesmen forgot his skill as a lawmaker who had forged a code for the nation, as a businessman whose establishments they frequented, as a victorious military chief with few peers. When McIntosh spoke, tribesmen listened, whether or not they agreed. Probably more damaging even than the Cherokee council incident, however, were the threats that Big Warrior now circulated against him in the Creek Nation.

When Secretary of War John C. Calhoun heard of Agent Crowell's and Sub-agent Walker's encouraging the Creeks to stand their ground and not sell land, he angrily dismissed Walker from his post and reprimanded Crowell for failure to cooperate with the commissioners. From then on, Crowell seems to have actively promoted Indian removal and to have encouraged cession of land. There were indications, however, that Crowell spoke against the removal behind the scenes.

On November 29, 1824, the Creek Nation's chiefs, headmen, and warriors met at the national council at Broken Arrow; negotiations began two days later. About two hundred chiefs of the nation and more than six thousand warriors were gathered. Big Warrior had done well his job of attacking McIntosh's integrity. The air was full of rumors about death to the chiefs who signed away land, whispered comments about McIntosh, and a continuing denial of the commissioners' demand to cede land. Chief McIntosh was keenly aware of the rumors but had determined that many of the chiefs and headmen who favored ceding land would do so in spite of the rumors of death.

McIntosh had been "broken" (dismissed) as speaker of the national council because of the accusations of President Ross and the Cherokee council.[18] McIntosh came before the national council and said that while Agent Mitchell was in power, he (McIntosh) had done as he pleased. Things were different now, however, and McIntosh said that he would not do anything of which the chiefs disapproved. Then the matter of Chief Ross's written accusations came before the council—accusations that McIntosh had offered land to the United States commissioners. McIntosh denied the charge, and Commissioner Campbell denied it, as well. Little Prince accepted the denials, and Chief McIntosh was reinstated as speaker.

As the council began talks with the commissioners, the discussions were put into writing to avoid misinterpretation. This proved to be slow, so the commissioners suggested oral negotiations. The chiefs agreed. McIntosh addressed the council, stating that the laws passed in council applied to all, even Big Warrior and Little Prince.

During the council proceedings, Commissioners Campbell and Meriwether arranged through Agent Crowell to obtain rations that Major John Brodnax was to disperse from an old local factory site to the Indians. Because of a steady stream of late arrivals, the commissioners had to order more food after the council got underway. On December 7 the peace pipe was passed, the hand of fellowship extended, and the commissioners presented their talks to the assembled chiefs. They told the chiefs that a bargain had been struck twenty years before, between the new government and Georgia, to clear the Indians from all lands in the state. As part of that agreement, the United States was to have purchased all lands in Georgia from the Indians. The chiefs were reminded that the white man surrounded them and that troubles had continued between Indians and whites. They were told that the president had a land west of the Mississippi and that he wished his "red children" to move there. The commissioners said that the removal would be long but the new land would be comfortable and secure.

The council continued the next day, the chiefs responding that they were not aware of any such twenty-year-old agreement. Any removal, they asserted, would be a hardship on the Creek nation. They wanted to know what assurances they would have against further encroachments by the white men if they agreed to removal. For each acre they ceded, the Creeks would receive an equal acre in the new territory to which they would remove. The whites promised to protect them from encroachments by new settlers. Finally, weighing these assurances against the hardships of removal, the chiefs agreed. Little Prince, Opothle Yoholo, William McIntosh, and Hopoy Hadgo signed the new agreement.

The intensity with which the subjects were discussed again prompted the recording of the talks, to lessen the chance of misinterpretation. On December 9 the commissioners presented their "talk" in writing. The Creeks were reminded that they had sided with the British and had suffered the same fate—defeat. Still, the new United States government had been kind and generous to the Creeks. The commissioners reminded the Indians that other tribes, such as the Delawares, the six nations of the Sioux, and the Cherokees, had fought with the British and had lost.

The commissioners declared that all these tribes had lost power after the American Revolution. Nevertheless, the government wished the Indians to live and prosper, to advance in civilization, to have good laws and obey them, and to have churches and schools. To attain these goals, the president wished them to go west, where there was plenty of game. They could cultivate the land and become herdsmen. The commissioners noted that the Cherokee had been urged to go. They warned the Creeks not to listen to the talk or follow the "pattern" of the Cherokees, as they had done at Tuckabatchee and Pole Cat Springs. Those "talks" had not been binding. The talk in the current council was binding on the whole nation. The Indians were reminded of the disastrous civil war that had nearly ruined their nation. The commissioners concluded by saying that the Congress of the United States and the Assembly of Georgia were in session and waiting for the outcome of the meeting.

Another twenty thousand rations were ordered that day, and at this point, the chiefs responded. They denied that their people had originally come from the West. Their tradition held that the soil and the land had always been theirs, for when the whites landed, the red men who met them were from Coweta towns. The chiefs added that the 1802 treaty had called for peaceful terms, which meant that they had the right of occupancy until they decided to dispose of the land.

Passionately, they proclaimed that each treaty, from New York in 1790, from Fort Jackson in 1814, and Indian Springs in 1821, had guaranteed them the remainder of their lands. The chiefs again stated that they had barely sufficient land left for the nation. The proposed removal was out of the question; their aged, sick, and young would never survive the trip. Little Prince signed as principal chief, Chief McIntosh as speaker of the Nation, Opothle Yoholo as speaker of the Upper Towns, and Hopoy Hadgo also signed the talks.

Governor Troup wrote to the commissioners, asking impatiently whether there were any signs of progress. The legislature was to adjourn in four days, and he hungered for news of a treaty that he could proclaim to the Georgia Assembly. The commissioners responded that heavy rains had delayed the meetings and that they had encountered obstacles that had put the signing of the treaty in question. They reported that the writing of the talks had been abandoned as too slow. They complained that the recalcitrant Cherokees had exerted a steady influence on the chiefs of the council. They also claimed that Big Warrior's threats against the chiefs of the Lower Towns were undermining the chiefs' willingness to cede land. Even McIntosh noted the number who had earlier been willing to negotiate but who were now afraid.

The commissioners had worked for a successful conclusion to a treaty, but the adamant opposition of the Upper Town chiefs offered little hope. On December 14 the chiefs assembled and several expressed their opinions with vehemence. The commissioners were then invited in; they spoke forcefully to the council about an exchange of all or part of the land. They urged the chiefs to conclude such a treaty and allow the Indians who were awaiting the outcome to go home. It would also save the government additional expense. All of these proposals were rejected. The commissioners refused to take no as a conclusive answer and asked to meet the next day.

On December 16 the commissioners again met the council and referred to former treaties at Augusta, Galphinton, and Shoulderbone, reminding the Creeks that the land held for them was simply hunting ground. Finally, in irritation, aged Little Prince stood. He informed the commissioners that his speakers had several times said no, but that the commissioners would not believe them. Now, to emphasize their position, he would declare it personally. At this point, the commissioners laid before the council documents of evidence favoring a claim by Blackburn and Houston of Tennessee against the Creeks. They then retired.

The commissioners renewed their demands for land in council on December 18. Big Warrior's deputy, Opothle Yoholo, rose and angrily stated that he would not take a house full of money for his interest in the land. The commissioners chose to retire from the council. They pondered their future course. They felt that they had been defeated by Big Warrior's repeated threats of death to those who sold or exchanged lands. Those threats had been repeated in all council talks. Weighing the determination of the Upper Town chiefs to hold land against the Lower Town chiefs' more agreeable attitude toward selling, the commissioners decided to negotiate only with the chiefs within the boundaries of Georgia.[19]

This seemed the only avenue left by which to attain a treaty. Commissioner Campbell had a conference with several chiefs of the Lower Towns to investigate the possibility of treating with them alone. The chiefs were generally willing but fearful of repeated death threats. Campbell approached Chief McIntosh and urged him to favor cession in open council, but the chief refused, knowing that his death would be the result.

Circumstances were drawing a web around McIntosh. If a treaty was to be attained, it would have to be concentrated on the chiefs of the Lower Towns, of whom McIntosh was the leader. Colonel William Williamson, employed by the commissioners to work with the council chiefs, was instructed to talk with McIntosh and several other chiefs. The theme of these talks was the determination of the United States to gain all remaining lands in Georgia east of the Chattahoochee River. It is probable that during these talks McIntosh's idea of removal returned to dominate his thoughts, for he well knew what would happen if the chiefs and warriors refused to go—near-genocide of the nation. Wistfully, he longed for the prewar days when Creeks and whites had mingled in relative peace. He knew the mind of the whites . . . and he had witnessed their insatiable greed for land.

McIntosh was persuaded to meet secretly with the commissioners in the woods near Broken Arrow. The chiefs in council got word of the meeting and passed a law against any chief who dealt with whites outside the council meetings.[20] This law was agreed to by the tribal council and directed mainly against McIntosh, who the chiefs feared was making a deal with the whites to cede land. To break this law meant a chief had gone against the best interests of the Creek Nation, so he must be "broken," or fired, from his senior tribal position. Little Prince then broke McIntosh as speaker of the nation, although he could not break him as chief because of his following among the chiefs and warriors of the Lower Towns.[21] McIntosh, deeply angered and humiliated, left immediately for Coweta, where he was guarded by his own warriors. A short time later, he went to his residence at Acorn Bluff.

The national council at Broken Arrow was temporarily adjourned. Commissioners Meriwether and Campbell went to Washington to present to the president the idea of negotiating with the Georgia chiefs only. The argument in favor of such a treaty was the commissioners' conviction that the chiefs of the Lower Towns were willing to sell the land that lay within the boundaries of Georgia. Chief McIntosh was consulted about the details and the consequences of this approach. The commissioners pointed out that McIntosh had been west and seen the land and the advantages of going there.[22] He was known to prefer the territory held by the Choctaws but held no further reservation about going west. If he and his people went, they would form the largest body of Indians there.

President Monroe declined Commissioner Campbell's suggestion of a treaty with Georgia chiefs alone, so Campbell proposed another alternative—negotiate with the Georgia chiefs, with the consent of the Upper Town chiefs, so that the land ceded would immediately revert to the United States. He submitted the idea to Secretary of War Calhoun before proposing it to the president. Apparently, Calhoun and the president agreed, for Campbell immediately instructed Agent Crowell to ask the chiefs of the nation to assemble at McIntosh's inn at Indian Springs on February 7, 1825.

President Monroe and Secretary Calhoun were trying to remove all barriers to a final treaty and sternly charged Crowell to actively aid the commissioners in their task. Indian Springs was chosen because the government believed that it could better protect Chief McIntosh and the Lower Town chiefs there.

The legal wedge that Big Warrior was using on McIntosh was an old law that proclaimed death to any chief who ceded more land. Tradition held that the chief himself had first proclaimed the law.[23] Although reenacted at Broken Arrow, the law was apparently never written by McIntosh when he coded the laws of the nation in 1817.

When McIntosh reached Coweta, the seat of his power and authority, he called for the chiefs and the headmen of the Lower Towns. When they gathered, he spoke to them of the American government's plans to acquire the rest of the land in Georgia and of the inevitable result for the Indians—either to die fighting a superior military force or to remove voluntarily to land west of the Mississippi:

> The white man is growing in the State of Georgia, he wants our lands, he will buy them now, but by and by he will take them and the little band of our people will be left to wander without homes, poor, despised, and beaten like dogs; we will go to our new homes, and learn like the white man to till the earth, grow cattle, and depend on these for food and life. Let us learn to make books like the white man does and we shall grow again into a Great Nation.[24]

Etomme Tustennuggee, a chief of Coweta, admitted that he had been duped into signing the Pole Cat Springs talk. Now he felt no obligation to abide by it. McIntosh persuaded him to support a treaty ceding the land that the commissioners wanted. Then the chief gathered around him the chiefs of the Lower Towns who favored such a cession and held council on January 25, 1825.[25] Chiefs gathered from Coweta, Talladega, Cussetta, Broken Arrow, and Hitchita. Little Prince, chief of Broken Arrow, was not present. Chief McIntosh and the council addressed a talk to President Monroe, laying before him the terrible difficulties that the Creek nation faced. They reminded the president that they had fought for the

United States in the last war against the Red Sticks. They said that the victorious chiefs, led by Chief McIntosh, held a position in the national council that was superior to the position of the defeated Red Sticks. (They noted that Gun Boy, once a leader of the Red Sticks, then a prisoner in the Florida campaign, now issued orders against the "friendly party" of Creeks.) They wrote that Big Warrior was holding council to lay plans to dismiss Chief McIntosh and his adherents. They also claimed that Crowell was partial to Big Warrior.

Thirty-six chiefs of the Lower Towns signed the agreement. McIntosh signed as speaker of the nation,[26] Chilly signed as clerk of the national council, and Samuel Hawkins was the interpreter. The same day, the chiefs also sent word to the president that Chief McIntosh and other chiefs would enter into a treaty with the commissioners in an exchange for lands west of the Mississippi. The tone of the talk and the fact that Chief McIntosh and Chilly signed according to their council roles left little doubt that they considered the council at Coweta equal in importance to the national council.

The United States commissioners arrived at Indian Springs on February 12, 1825, for the next attempt at a treaty.[27] Agent Crowell sent the commissioners a note assuring them of his full cooperation, and Campbell and Meriwether sent a message to Governor Troup that the end of the Indian occupation in Georgia had nearly come.

During the Broken Arrow council, McIntosh had noted a hesitancy in those chiefs who had once declared a willingness to cede land. Now, at Indian Springs, he continued to promote the land cession among his people and carefully assured the chiefs of their superior position in the council as victors over the Red Sticks. The Lower Town chiefs and headmen were amenable to land cessions, but threats of death had been spread so assiduously by Big Warrior that anticipation was mixed with an atmosphere of foreboding. This atmosphere became tinged with fear as the Indians of the Upper Towns pitched their tents on the north side of Indian Springs and painted the rocks near them red—the color of war.

On Thursday, February 10, the commissioners, noting that approximately four hundred chiefs and headmen had arrived, gave the Indians notice to meet them in council at noon. Then the chiefs of the Upper Towns, from Tuckabatchee, responded that they were not ready and that they wanted to meet at their camp rather than in the large room that the commissioners had arranged for. The commissioners demanded that the council begin in the designated room.

Campbell faced the gathered chiefs and headmen and began in a now familiar way. He talked in a friendly manner about removal to a good land at a fork of the Arkansas and the Canadian rivers. He spoke of the advantages—that the Indians would be left alone by whites and protected from intruders. The president wanted his red children to go; they were not to listen to the Cherokee talk. The Creeks remembered how they had fought with the British against the rebellious colonists. When the colonists won the war for independence the president of the new republic looked protectively on the Indians. They were now subject to him. The Creeks had signed a treaty of peace, and now wanted to keep that peace. However, as the commissioners had again and again negotiated for land, the chiefs now realized that the remaining land was all they had left. With mixed feelings they were asked to surrender to the wishes of the president.

When Campbell finished, Agent Crowell stood before the chiefs and urged them to go west, adding that he had not been instructed to advise them at Broken Arrow and had thus remained silent. The talk of Broken Arrow was repeated, and $400,000 was to be given to the Indians to cover the loss of improvements and the expenses of removal. The commissioners asked the chiefs to meet at noon the next day, and then retired.

The chiefs and headmen of the Lower Towns met that evening in their own council and discussed the proposals fully. McIntosh undoubtedly actively urged removal. The greatest number of representatives were from the oldest towns in the nation, Coweta and Cussetta. Finally, a vote was taken: all but two favored ceding land.

The next day, the commissioners met the chiefs at noon in a large room. The chiefs of the Upper and Lower Towns, who had met in different groups the previous evening, now spoke as two voices in the council. At this council, several eloquent speeches were delivered by the Indians. McIntosh addressed the assembled chiefs and headmen. Also present were Cherokee Chiefs Major Ridge and John Ross, who sided with and influenced the chiefs of the Upper Towns in opposing the treaty. Opothle Yoholo led the opposition. General McIntosh spoke for about two hours. In part, he said:

> This mighty nation has become dwarfed, and it will only be a matter of time when there will be no game in the country, and they will be without food. Some of the young men have been to the proffered land beyond the Great River. It is good and the game is abundant. Will you stay and die with them here and leave no one to follow you, or come to your grave and weep over their chief. Beyond the Great River is the bright sun and the sky as blue and the water as sweet as they are here. Our people will go with us. To love the ground is mean; to love the people is noble.[28]

When he finished, the braves responded with approval. Opothle Yoholo, who had replaced McIntosh as speaker of the nation at Broken Arrow, stood to speak. Looking at the commissioners, he spoke with a determined, persuasive urgency:

> We met you at Broken Arrow, and then told you we had no land to sell. I then heard of no claims against the Nation, nor have I since. We have met you here at very short notice, and do not think the chiefs who are here have any authority to treat. General McIntosh knows that we are bound by our laws, and that what is not done in public square in general council, is not binding on the whole Nation. I am, therefore, under the necessity of repeating the same answer as given at Broken Arrow, that we have no land to sell. I know that there are but a few from the Upper towns here, and many are absent from the Lower towns. General McIntosh knows that no land can be sold without full council, and without the consent of the full Nation; and, if a part of the Nation chose to leave the country, they cannot sell the land they have, but it belongs to the nation. From what you have told us today, I

am induced to believe it is best for us to remove, but we must have time to think of it; and, should the chiefs here sell the land now, it might create dissension and ill blood among the Indians. I have received a message from my head Chief, Big Warrior, directing me to listen to what the Commissioners say, to meet them friendly, and part in the same way, but not to sell land. I am also instructed to invite you to meet us at Broken Arrow three months hence, when a treaty may be made, and to return home. This is the only talk I have for you, and I shall return home immediately. I gave you but one talk at Broken Arrow, and I shall give you but one talk here. Such is the message I have received from my Chief, and I am bound to obey; tomorrow I shall leave here. I have now said all I have to say; I will listen to any thing further you have to say, but I shall give no further answer.[29]

Chief McIntosh stood, looking first at Opothle Yoholo, and spoke with intensity to the members of the council. He said, with firmness and evenness of voice, that the present council was authorized to make a treaty and should do so. A heated discussion ensued, with other chiefs rising in turn to give their views. The commissioners decided to leave the council so that the Indians could speak freely among themselves. Finally, the council broke up, unresolved.

Saturday morning, the commissioners were told that a part of the Cussetta and the Soowagaloo tribal parties had left rather mysteriously during the night.[30] Following an investigation, the commissioners heard from a half-breed that Colonel William Hamby had ordered the Indians to leave.[31] There was evidence that Colonel William Stedham and Opothle Yoholo had ordered the Cussetta chiefs to return to their homes.[32] Those chiefs had been known to favor signing the treaty. Stunned by the leaving of two chiefs, Campbell and Meriwether called the council to meet at 2 P.M. to sign the treaty. Opothle Yoholo did not leave, as he had said that he would, but stayed around and spoke against the treaty at every opportunity. His oratorical brilliance shone as he spoke in council, but his incisive attempts at persuasion did not deter the remaining chiefs and headmen, who wanted the signing to proceed. His delegation, under orders from Big Warrior, refused to sign. A chief from Talladega did not sign. Etomme Tustennuggee, a chief from Coweta, began the parade of signers. Chief McIntosh was next. At the moment that he took the pen in his hand, Opothle Yoholo, standing with a group of Indians outside the inn, jumped on a rock and angrily pointed a finger at the chief, who stood, visible through the window, bent to sign. Yoholo accused McIntosh of being double-tongued and shouted that he would die in his own blood.[33] McIntosh looked out the window at Yoholo, standing like an animated statue on the rock, then signed and encouraged others to do so.

The treaty provided $400,000 to the Creek nation: $200,000 when the United States Congress ratified the treaty and the rest in annual installments for the next five years. The greatest part of the remaining Creek territory in Georgia and a part of Alabama were ceded to the United States, specifically, the land between the Flint and the Chattahoochee rivers, and the land on the Tallapoosa and the Coosa rivers. These lands were ceded for lands of equal acreage and value in Arkansas (later Oklahoma). The Creeks were promised help with farming techniques and protection both from whites encroaching on their land and Indian rebels from neighboring tribes.

An amendment was later added, giving Chief McIntosh $25,000 for his home on the Chattahoochee and his Indian Springs home. He was probably also given money to sign the treaty.[34] When Crowell, who was not in the room at the time, heard of the amendment, he was visibly angry. The agent wrote to Secretary of War Calhoun that only McIntosh and his adherents had signed the treaty and that it did not comply with government instructions because the chiefs of the Upper Towns had not signed. Crowell knew that President Monroe had insisted that the whole Creek Nation agree to the spirit of the treaty, so he left for Washington to object to the document personally.

After the treaty-signing formalities were concluded, Chief McIntosh, Etomme Tustennuggee, and other chiefs of the Lower Towns journeyed east, to the state capital at Milledgeville, to talk with the governor about the treaty and removal. They were also fearful that the threats made against the signers of the treaty by Big

Opothle Yoholo warns McIntosh not to sign the treaty.

Warrior and the chiefs of the Upper Towns would be carried out. But Governor Troup assured them of the state's protection and sent his aide-de-camp, Colonel Henry G. Lamar, to both Cussetta and Tuckabatchee to sound out how the chiefs of the Upper Towns felt toward those who had signed the treaty. Colonel Lamar sternly warned Big Warrior and the other chiefs against any punitive measures toward McIntosh and the chiefs of the Lower Towns.

Agent Crowell had, in the meantime, gone to Washington to protest the treaty. He was cautious at first but quickly escalated his warnings against the treaty when he realized that President Monroe's days in office were coming to an end. The president did not choose to deal with so hot an issue and passed it on to Congress. He did not even read Crowell's letter protesting the treaty. The treaty was ratified early in March by the United States Senate and approved by newly elected President John Quincy Adams.[35]

As Colonel Lamar returned from his mission to the chiefs of the Upper Towns, he informed Governor Troup that the Creeks would submit peacefully to the treaty. It had been approved by the president, and Little Prince and other chiefs expressed confidence that their father, the president, would protect them. The Indians had an almost childlike confidence in the wisdom, virtue, and power of the president.

Big Warrior, the lately absent power of resistance to all further land concessions, had apparently died after Colonel Lamar's mission. Into the leadership vacancy stepped Opothle Yoholo.

Chief McIntosh went to Acorn Bluff, secure in Governor Troup's promise of protection. The United States commissioners had also promised government protection, so the chief did not alert his own warriors to take safety measures while he stayed there.

As soon as the treaty was ratified, Governor Troup and Chief McIntosh exchanged letters about the surveying of the newly ceded land. Troup, up for election for the first time in 1825, urgently wanted the lands opened for white settlement. In agreement with the governor, the chief set up an office for lottery signers at Acorn Bluff. Georgians and others who wanted prime Indian lands rushed to sign up.

On April 12, 1825, aware that the time of removal to the lands beyond the Mississippi was near, Chief McIntosh and the chiefs and the headmen of the Lower Towns sent a "Memorial" to the Georgia legislature by way of Governor Troup. Probably composed by the chief, it was written in the official flowery language of the day and spoke of the Great Spirit as having given land to his "red children." It said that the Indians were as numerous as the trees of the forests. When the white man came from across the great waters, the forefathers of the Creeks offered the pipe of peace and friendship. The white man soon became as numerous as the trees and wanted more land; the whites became "like a mighty storm" and "tore us up by the root." The white friends had promised their red brothers a better land.

They spoke of "taking the talk" of President Washington and others in Virginia after the Revolutionary War. The chiefs expressed their faith in the United States presidents as advisors and protectors and felt satisfied with the advice of the commissioners about ceding the land in Georgia. They thanked the United States and Georgia for many presents and for having taught them the use of the loom, the plow, and the hoe. They thanked the assembly for teaching the values of different kinds of property. Finally, they wrote:

> Brothers and friends we have to part from you. You are shortly to be the possessors of our land, and our homes. Homes dear to us because we were raised and nourished in them. Our food is plain and wholesome, and affords us support and health. Our people are thinly clothed, our huts shelter them from cold. We have enjoyed in a considerable degree many of the comforts of life, rendered [familiar] to us by our intercourse with our white friends, and to a much greater extent than a people like us can again shortly expect. When we are removed to the wilderness of the west, Friends and brothers, all of the comfort we now enjoy we must abandon for your sakes, our wives and helpless children must experience fatigue and hunger, cold and every other incident that must unavoidably attend us in our travel from this late beloved country to the western wilderness, full of dangers that we prob-

ably do not foresee. But we put our trust in the Great Spirit and our Father, the President, for protection and aid.[36]

The memorial was signed by sixteen chiefs and read to a special assembly of the Georgia legislature on May 23, 1825.

As soon as the surveyors began their work on the newly ceded lands, the chiefs of the Upper Towns held council in Tuckabatchee. Little Prince, chief of Broken Arrow and principal chief of the Creek Nation, had aligned himself with the Upper Towns on the issue of the treaty. These chiefs met several times to discuss the effects of the Indian Springs treaty on the nation, of losing more land to the whites, and of watching the surveyor's chain being drawn across farms and hunting grounds. No single act better symbolized the white man's greed for Indian land than did the stretch of the surveyor's chain. Yoholo recounted how he had warned McIntosh and the other chiefs and headmen from the Lower Towns not to sign but that McIntosh had urged the gathered chiefs to cede the land. Feelings against McIntosh quickly dominated the meetings, along with the judgment that the nation's law had been "broken" and must now be "mended" (satisfied, justice done).

Agent Crowell, attending the council, seems to have promoted the notion of mending the broken law by killing McIntosh.[37] The council members demanded the deaths of McIntosh, his son Chilly, Etomme Tustennuggee, Joseph Miller, Joseph Marshall, Samuel Hawkins, and James Island, all signers of the treaty.[38] Little Prince then called for the death of Chief McIntosh to mend the law. He seems to have given consent to the younger chiefs, who now ruled the Upper Towns and dominated the council. The old chief knew that he would never leave the land of his fathers; in his eyes was the twilight of life's sunset.

The council urged Menawa to lead the execution party. He at first refused, although acknowledging his hatred of McIntosh. The council insisted, however, and Menawa finally accepted. Two other leaders, Itcockchungo and Thlococosmicco, agreed to go as commanders with Menawa.

IV

The Death
of McIntosh

Menawa, whose longstanding thirst for revenge might now be realized, looked over the gathering of warriors. The mangled veteran knew his men and began selecting those who would go. About one hundred and seventy warriors from Okfuskee and Tuckabatchee, under the leadership of Menawa and Tuckeehadjo, were chosen. A white man, Jim Hutton, was asked to accompany the party.[1] He had grown up in the Creek Nation and was accepted as one of their own. He spoke English and could assure any whites whom the party encountered that they would not be harmed. The party proceeded toward the east, one man behind the other, moving quietly and invisibly through the forests toward Acorn Bluff.

The death sentence was supposed to be secret, lest the offender flee. But whispers of the council's decision soon spread through the countryside. Chilly McIntosh, at his home at Broken Arrow, received word of the council's intention and immediately dispatched a runner to warn his father, urging him to leave the house.[2] For some reason, perhaps because of the promised protection of United States Commissioners Campbell and Meriwether and Governor Troup, McIntosh felt safe and remained at his home on the Chattahoochee. Strangely, he did not even alert his own warriors to the possibility of danger.

The party arrived at a place near Acorn Bluff on the second day, the afternoon of May 30, 1825, and hid in the woods near McIntosh's home. The clouds that had brought torrential rains had broken up. Just below the plantation, the swollen Chattahoochee River rushed past its tree-lined banks. Voices were heard in the two-story log house where the chief and his family lived; and at that moment, McIntosh and Sam Hawkins (an old friend and his son-in-law), emerged from the house. They mounted horses and slowly headed down the road toward Hawkins' home. A little way down the road, the chief bade Samuel farewell until the next day, when they were to begin a journey west to inspect the new land.

One chief and a detachment of warriors were dispatched to follow Hawkins to his home. They were to hold him until word came of McIntosh's death, then kill Hawkins.

The warriors could easily have killed McIntosh then, but they remained hidden in the foliage. They had been instructed to kill the chief according to Creek custom—on the offender's property, in the presence of his family. In the few hours of daylight that remained, the warriors quietly gathered wood into three large bundles and chose strong men to carry them. Then they waited.

In the darkness of the next morning, the warriors advanced quietly toward the two-story house where McIntosh's family and friends slept and placed the bundles of firewood at the foundation. Fire was struck in the wood, and the armed warriors took positions around the house. Flames were soon crackling, outlining the house against the night.

Light from the fire illuminated the guest house in the yard nearby as several warriors and Jim Hutton broke open the door to the guest house. Two men looked up from their beds, bewildered by the painted faces of the warriors who had burst so suddenly into their room. Both men looked white, but the man in the bed to the left had peddler's wares piled on the floor beside the bed, so Hutton and the warriors approached him, probably to assure him that he would not be harmed. At that moment, the other "white" man, Chilly McIntosh, bolted from his bed and jumped out the window. Both warriors ran outside and fired at him, but his movements were too quick. Knowing the land and every tree intimately, he ran down the hill and jumped into the rushing Chattahoochee, swam through the cold, black waters, and escaped to the other side.

Meanwhile, the peddler hastily got up, dressed, grabbed his

merchandise, and left the guest house. He stared briefly at the main house, where the flames had reached the second story, and at the circle of warriors around it. Fire was then set to the guest house, and it roared brightly into the night sky.

The main house puffed billows of smoke, and tongues of fire leaped through windows and doors, casting eerie lights and shadows behind the warriors surrounding it. The wives, Susannah and Peggy McIntosh, appeared at the door with their children. Warriors dragged them into the yard and stripped the children naked. Susannah begged for the life of McIntosh, but Menawa ignored her plea. The crusty survivor of Horseshoe Bend smiled at McIntosh's predicament. He had dreamed of this moment. Remembering, he gently rubbed the hideous scar on his cheek.

Menawa yelled, "McIntosh, we have come. We have come. We told you if you sold the land to the government, we would come."[3] The warriors yelled war cries in chorus to the old chief's proclamation.

Chief McIntosh threw his weight against the door to hold it closed against the young warriors who attempted to enter the house. A guest and longtime friend, Etomme Tustennuggee, an older chief of Coweta, brought guns for himself and for McIntosh. Smoke curled through the log floor, filling the room. Shots coming through the windows smashed into the walls. Finding it difficult to breathe, Chief McIntosh suddenly swung open the door, and he and Etomme fired at the circle of warriors. A volley of shots poured through the open doorway, and Etomme fell to the floor, dead. McIntosh fired again, then retreated upstairs with several guns. He continued to fire at the warriors from the windows, but the smoke and the heat forced him back downstairs. He fired again from the bottom step; then a half-dozen shots bit into his flesh. McIntosh fell and was dragged by his feet down the steps and into the yard. With great effort, he lifted himself on an elbow and looked defiantly into the face of his attacker. The warrior raised a long dagger into the air, then plunged it, up to the hilt, into the chief's chest. Chief McIntosh sighed heavily and died. The warrior swiftly scalped the chief, giving a war cry as he raised his bloody hand in triumph.

The raiding party killed the hogs and burned the crops of corn,

Menawa and warriors as they move to kill McIntosh.

beans, and melons. Then they tied up the Negro slaves, roped the horses and the cows, and led them away. Before the warriors left, Peggy begged them for a burial suit for McIntosh, but they refused.

When the warriors who were holding Sam Hawkins at his home heard of McIntosh's death, they killed the half-breed chief, who had also signed the treaty, and threw his body into the Talla-poosa River.

As the dawn seeped quietly through the trees, only the smok-ing outlines of houses remained. Dead animals cluttered the farm's planting ground, which lay alongside the river. Susannah and Peggy, in shock from the attack, numbly gathered their naked children and headed for the safety of neighbors' houses.

V

The Creeks
Move West

A FEW weeks after the death of McIntosh, the chief's elder son, Chilly, returned to the Creek Nation and received permission from Little Prince to reside there. This permission was necessary because the old chief had previously supported the order for Chilly to be killed. Peggy, stunned by the killing of her husband by warriors of his own tribe, returned sadly to her native Cherokee Nation. The chief's other widows, Eliza and Susannah, along with their children, quietly resumed their lives among the Creeks.

On June 29, 1825, the Creek Nation pardoned the remaining members of the McIntosh family and friends, and Little Prince urged them to return to the nation. He called them unfortunate and misguided and promised them protection under the Creek law. On July 25 Opothle Yoholo, Little Prince, and other chiefs signed over the Indian Springs property to McIntosh, as stipulated in the treaty of 1821. This presumably went to Chief William's heirs.

The U. S. government met with the chiefs and warriors of the Creek Nation in Washington on January 24, 1826. The assembled delegation voided the treaty made in Indian Springs the previous February, because they did not believe the signers were authorized to cede land on behalf of the Indian nation. The new treaty also ceded the remaining land in Georgia to the United States.

Article 10 of the treaty authorized the listing of the damages to the property of Chief McIntosh, Chilly, members of the McIntosh family, and several of their friends who suffered losses at the hands of the hostile Creek party. General Edmund Gaines asked Chilly for the list, and required the Creek Nation to pay for the damages.

A comparison of the treaties of 1825 and 1826 points up the importance of timing as it affects the readiness of both parties to negotiate. Opothle Yoholo, speaking for the Upper Creeks and the principal chief, had urged more time be given the Indians to sign during the Indian Springs talks. At that time he angrily denounced the treaty being signed there. Later in Washington, he and the other chiefs of the Creeks signed what was basically the same treaty.

Four hundred thousand dollars was to be paid to the Creek Nation in the 1825 treaty, but only $217,000 was paid in the 1826 treaty. The land considered in both treaties lay west, northwest, and north of the state of Georgia. In the treaty of 1825 the line ran from the "principal falls" on the Chattahoochee River, "above Coweta, to Okfuskee Old Town, upon the Tallapoosa, thence to the falls on Coosaw river, at or near a place called the Hickory Ground." It is not clear where the principal falls is, but it seems to run generally west and north, along the western edge of the state of Georgia. The treaty of 1826 describes the line as running from the Chattahoochee River fifty miles below the boundary of the Creek and Cherokee nations, near Buzzard's Roost, to forty-five miles west of Buzzard's Roost.

Signers of both treaties included Tuskeegee Tustunnuggee, of the Lower Creeks, and John Crowell, as Indian agent.

Of interest is John Ridge, who witnessed the signing as secretary of the Creek Nation. John, a Cherokee, was the son of Major Ridge. Another Cherokee, David Vann, also witnessed the treaty.

The two leaders of the war party that killed McIntosh, Opothle Yoholo and Menawa, signed. Only Timpoochee Barnard and Tuskeegee Tustunnuggee are recognizable as Lower Creek chiefs in the delegation.

Under the 1825 treaty, the Indians were allowed a year and a half for removal to the West; for the treaty of 1826, one year. This clearly indicates the haste of the United States to rid Georgia of all its native sons.

Haste was apparently also involved in the agreement of the treaty of 1826, which was meant to cede all remaining Creek lands

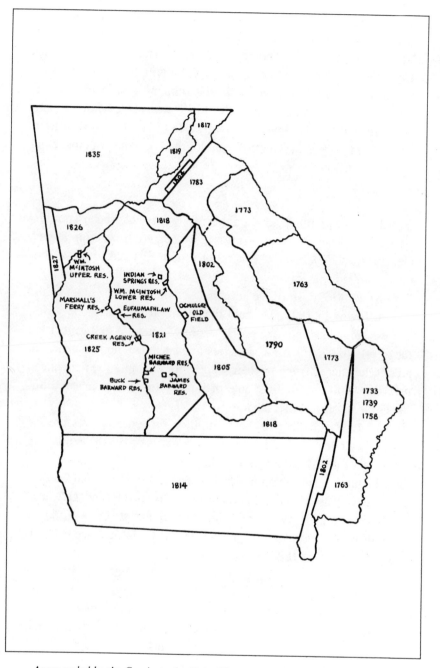

Areas ceded by the Creeks to the United States government, 1733–1827. This map shows treaty lines as originally drawn.

in Georgia. Somehow the lines which the U.S. government and Creek delegations had agreed on did not include a narrow strip of land in the northwest corner of Georgia. The U.S. government asked the Creek chiefs to meet them at Wetumph, an Indian town, on November 15, 1827, to cede that remaining strip of land. In weary resignation the ailing Little Prince was helped from a hammock so that he could sign the treaty. He died a few weeks afterward. The fiery orator, Opothle Yoholo, then became principal chief of the Creek Nation.

. . .

By 1825, Chilly, now a chief of Coweta, had been commissioned a major in the U.S. Army. He welcomed the visiting French General de Lafayette to Creek country with fifty naked and elaborately painted warriors.

Roley McIntosh, the chief's half-brother, became chief of the Lower Towns in 1828. He held that position for thirty-one years, and was an able administrator. His word was law. At first he resisted the efforts of Christian missionaries to evangelize the Indians, even though he shared some of their values; for example, he denounced polygamy and opposed the sale of liquor. Roley later married Susannah, one of the chief's widows.

In 1828, yielding to the continuing government pressure for removal, Chilly obtained a small ship and boarded the remaining members of the McIntosh family, along with some other Creek families, including the Benjamin Perrymans, the Winsletts, and the Porters. The heads of these families were also chiefs and had been supporters of Chief William. The ship landed at Three Forks, a short distance north of the present-day city of Muskogee, Oklahoma, in February 1828.

. . .

A proper assessment of Chief William McIntosh must include a historical perspective of the attitudes of the chiefs and headmen a decade after the chief's death. Following his execution, Creeks of the Lower Towns began the removal to land beyond the Mississippi. Parts of the five major tribes in the Southeast made the "Trail of

Tears" trek: Cherokee, Creek, Choctaw, Chickasaw, and Seminole. The Cherokees, who had been angered by McIntosh's offer of money to the council, split into two parties, just as the Creeks did. Those favoring removal were led by Chiefs Elias Boudinot, Major Ridge, and John Waite. The party that had resisted removal was led by Chief John Ross. Boudinot, Ridge, and Waite were killed for their part in encouraging removal.

Before his death, Elias Boudinot said, "McIntosh was right, and was misunderstood. I had been controlled by Ross but I wish I had stood up for McIntosh instead of obeying Ross."[1] John Ridge, son of Major Ridge, said, "I am sorry that I let John Ross get me to speak evil of Chief McIntosh before he was murdered."[2] General Daniel Newnan of the Georgia militia called McIntosh a victim of manifest destiny. Having known both Chief McGillivray and Chief McIntosh, he considered McIntosh the greater of the two.[3] Indian Agent John Crowell called McIntosh a traitor to his people because McIntosh pursued the treaty of 1825 at Indian Springs. After McIntosh met the Cherokees at New Echota, Big Warrior plotted the demise of the chief's influence. General Thomas Woodward, who had fought with McIntosh, held him in the highest esteem.

There is evidence that McIntosh received money to sign the Indian Springs treaty of 1825 and was a recipient of the annuities that were part of the treaty. Money and materials were always a part of the bargaining in treaties. Cherokee chiefs before John Ross's time were bribed by United States officials to cede land. That may be one reason that Ross was so sensitive to the offer from McIntosh. Chief McGillivray and other chiefs of the Creek Nation were also secretly given money in Washington for land ceded.[4] Bribes can never be called right, but in fairness to McIntosh, historians must acknowledge the frequency with which this happened in government-Indian relations, rather than singling out Chief McIntosh as a lone culprit. With one possible exception, the money that McIntosh received was shared with other Indians.

Perhaps the most interesting view came from McIntosh's old archrival, Menawa. About ten years after he and another chief had led the execution party to kill McIntosh, emotions had had time to cool, allowing a change of heart. The old chief then spoke from a different perspective. At the council of Sechalitchar in 1835, as he listened to Opothle Yoholo, who was then principal chief, Menawa became very angry and stood to address him.

Holding up his hands, he said, "Here are the hands stained with the blood of McIntosh, and I am now ready to stain them again with the blood of his enemies, and those who made me a dupe of their foul designs. When I done the deed I thought I was right, but I am sorry."[5] Later, in 1836, the old chief, wearing the full uniform of a United States army officer, led Creek warriors against rebel Seminoles. When Woodward wrote about this council incident, he mentioned that Menawa had let out the secret about the McIntosh affair but never explained what the secret was.

Chief McIntosh has been called, among other epithets, hero, traitor, patriot, and self-serving. None of these do him justice. He was far more talented, more complex, and more versatile than these labels indicate. His life was the scenario of a multitalented man who reached into the events of both early American and Indian life, exhibiting ability in many areas. Next to that singular genius of the Cherokees, Sequoyah, whose syllabary made that nation literate, McIntosh was probably the most able Indian of the southeastern tribes.

Whatever conclusions we draw about the life of Chief William McIntosh, there is no question that his mark will remain forever on the pages of Georgia's history.

EPILOGUE
About That "Treasure"

THE Indian treasure we heard about at school is still part of the folklore of Carroll County, where it apparently started. In my travels to learn about Chief McIntosh, his life and times, I talked with persons from all over the county, all of whom had heard about the treasure, had heard about it all their lives, but knew no details.

I discussed McIntosh and the treasure with several historians who are familiar with Georgia's past. They were well acquainted with the chief and had heard of the treasure. The late Dr. J. C. Bonner, formerly professor of history, who has written several chapters on McIntosh, doubted the existence of the treasure. Bonner, who probably knew as much as anyone about the chief, seemed to feel that Menawa's party took everything valuable, including any treasure. If the chief had buried it, the family, particularly Chilly, would have known where.

There are two reasons that I believe no treasure was hidden by McIntosh—on the reserve or anywhere else. First, McIntosh family tradition does not support it. In my conversations with Chief W. E. "Dode" McIntosh, retired principal chief of the Creek Nation and great-grandson of the subject of this book, he has denied knowing anything about it. "Why didn't he tell Chilly about it?" Dode repeatedly asked. Second, historical research does not provide sufficient clues pointing to a treasure of the size reported in treasure magazines and books. William McIntosh was one of the wealthiest Indians in the Creek Nation: he had at least three wives and a dozen known children, operated two ferries, and owned several homes, an inn, a tavern, a trading post, slaves, and livestock. Small bills were probably paid in coin, but larger amounts, such as those from treaties, were probably paid in scrip or bank drafts. When the warriors arrived, they killed the chiefs and stripped the children of their clothing. They took the horses and probably the cattle, killed the rest of the livestock, and burned the food supply. Having taken everything of value and having burned what they could not take, the warriors left the remaining McIntosh family members destitute and helpless.

Had there been any treasure, surely McIntosh's survivors would have found it and used it.

APPENDIX I

Chief William McIntosh: A Summary of His Achievements

Businessman

McIntosh early manifested a leaning toward trade by selling beef to the army when he was about nineteen years old. He developed an ability that was astute but an attitude that was in some ways unfair. For example, while he was in charge of distributing annuities and owned a trading post, he forced the Indians to spend the full amount for merchandise. He gave no change. When John Crowell became agent, he took the distribution of annuities away from the chief. Crowell's brother, Thomas, opened a post in competition with McIntosh. The agent would pay the annuities only in large bills, forcing the Indians to buy more than they needed. McIntosh retaliated by cutting his prices.

In addition to his trading post, McIntosh owned taverns and several homes with Negro slaves who farmed the land and cared for the livestock. He built an inn in Indian Springs, which catered to the flow of travelers exploring Indian lands. At Coweta, McIntosh operated a ferry that carried passengers across the Chattahoochee. At the time of his death, he was one of the wealthiest Indians in the Creek Nation.

Military Commander

When the Red Sticks' War broke out, McIntosh was commissioned a major in the army, commanding an attachment of warriors.

Several chiefs of the Creek Confederacy were commissioned, but none higher than major. McIntosh not only demonstrated bravery in battles and skirmishes but won the admiration of General John Floyd at the battle of Autassee. Later, at the battle of Horseshoe Bend, he won high praise from General Jackson. He was the only Indian chief specifically mentioned for bravery and leadership in the general's report of that battle. As the campaign moved into the Deep South and northern Florida, McIntosh was promoted to brigadier general,[1] commanding a brigade of warriors. McIntosh was the only Indian so promoted in the Southeast and the only one to engage in hand-to-hand combat. His report on the Chehehaw Affair was the first field report written by an Indian in the army.[2]

Writer of Laws

McIntosh was the first Indian to codify Creek laws, in an effort to make them apply to both the Indian and the white cultures.[3] When we consider that McIntosh was not a trained lawyer, we realize that this was no small accomplishment. As one of the few men who understood the thoughts and feelings of both cultures, he was in a position to write laws to help the Creeks live with whites.

Family Man

McIntosh had at least three wives and twelve children. He seems to have been a good husband and a good provider. Jane and Chilly, the two oldest children, were sent to school in Milledgeville to learn to read and write English. Because the school was run by whites, they also learned how the white man thought. Two of McIntosh's wives, Susannah and Peggy, lived together at Acorn Bluff, apparently in harmony.

Man of Two Worlds

Chief McIntosh early came into favor with both Indians and whites. He cultivated the friendship of the white leaders he came to know and learned to speak and write English rather well. He realized that the influence of American culture was stronger than that of the Indian culture and that the Creeks were in many ways dependent on the Americans. For this reason he began to urge an assimilation of the cultures to save what remained of the Creek culture, an idea with which few agreed.

McIntosh came to know and admire General Daniel Newnan of the Georgia militia, even naming a son for him. McIntosh was an early confidant of Agent Benjamin Hawkins and reported the early movements of the Red Sticks to him.

As a warrior chief subordinate to Menawa before the war, he obtained permission to pursue and execute Indians who had killed whites. Big Warrior first came to resent McIntosh at the treaty of Fort Jackson, where McIntosh wielded an already formidable influence and power.

Yoholo Micco, a chief of the Upper Town, served with McIntosh against the rebels. He was one of the few who came to favor immigration to the West and who lost his position as chief of Eufaulu town because of it. Opothle Yoholo and Little Prince were admirers and supporters of McIntosh, an allegiance that changed before the council at Tuckabatchee. McIntosh had lived relatively comfortably in both cultures until then.

With the Americans' drive for land beyond the frontier, that comfortable relationship came to an abrupt end. McIntosh was caught between the Creek stance of holding all remaining land and the obviously stronger American might to take it. There is evidence that Opothle Yoholo's feelings of friendship continued until the treaty of 1825 at Indian Springs. Yoholo seems to have agreed with McIntosh that removal was inevitable but to have disagreed about the timing. In retrospect, McIntosh was ahead of his time.

United States Commissioner Campbell considered McIntosh the only Indian who understood correctly the relationship between the Creeks and the United States. Agent Crowell hated the chief for business and personal reasons. There is evidence that his influence and behind-the-scenes maneuvers contributed to the chief's death.

Evidence of the two worlds is seen in McIntosh's two residences. At Acorn Bluff, his main residence was mostly Creek in style and furnishings. Indian Springs, his summer residence, clearly contained the trappings of the postcolonial American culture—a piano, art, and the dining room furniture of the white culture.

APPENDIX II

The Family Carries On

McIntosh family leadership continued in the affairs of the Creek Nation as Indians moved west to Oklahoma territory. The missionary efforts of the Baptists had, by 1849, reached deeply into the ranks of the Creek warriors. Six of them, including William McIntosh's son Chilly, became preachers. These pastors were credited with raising the morale of the Creek Nation and helping to suppress the liquor traffic.

Roley McIntosh retired as chief in 1859. He had a sprawling ranch and farm worked by Negro slaves, and by this time had joined the Baptist church.

When the Civil War broke out, Chilly's brother Daniel Newnan McIntosh organized the First Creek Indian Confederate Regiment and served as its colonel. Chilly was commissioned as colonel of the Second Creek Regiment. Both regiments fought at the battles of Round Mountain, Pea Ridge in Arkansas, and Honey Springs. At Round Mountain they fought the Union Creeks under the command of Opothle Yoholo. During the Civil War the Upper Creeks favored the Union, while the Lower Creeks fought for the Confederacy.

Roley McIntosh died in 1863, at the home of his niece, Delilah, a daughter of Chief William McIntosh. The war devastated Roley's farm and his wealth. Before the Civil War the McIntosh family had been among the wealthiest in the Creek Nation.

Daniel Newnan established his home near present-day Fame, in McIntosh County, Oklahoma. He married Jane Ward and had four sons, Albert Gallatin, Freeland, Roley, and Daniel Newnan, Jr. Daniel Newnan McIntosh, Sr., was well educated and served as clerk of the council of the Lower Creeks. He organized the first Creek regiment for the Confederacy and was also a member of the Creek House of Warriors from 1887 to 1891. He recovered from the losses occasioned by the war, and became a successful farmer and stockraiser. He died at his farm near Fame on April 10, 1896. During his lifetime he had held every office except principal chief of the Creek Nation.

Daniel Newnan's eldest son, Albert Gallatin McIntosh, was born in Indian territory on January 27, 1848. He was educated at a school in Jefferson, Oklahoma, and then moved to Tennessee. Albert practiced law, and was elected school superintendent of Smith County. He married Mollie Boulton, a white woman, and had four sons, Freeland, Van, Daniel, and Waldo. He died on August 5, 1915.

Waldo Emerson ("Dode") McIntosh, the youngest son of Albert, met Lulu Vance early in life and married her as soon as they were of age. They had been married nearly seventy-one years when she died at age ninety-three in 1986. Dode still lives in Tulsa, Oklahoma. He was elected county treasurer of Tulsa, Oklahoma, and has also served as city clerk of Checotah, Oklahoma, county tax assessor, and president of the Intertribal Council. He was five-times principal chief of the Creek Nation, from 1961 to 1971.

Dode and Lulu had five children: Waldo E., Jr., was stationed at Moffett Field, California, during World War II and was killed in a flight-training accident; William V. is retired and living in Tulsa, Oklahoma; Mrs. Wilfred M. Lee lives with her husband in Riverton, Wyoming; Nocus H. is retired and lives near Jay, Oklahoma. Chinnubbie McIntosh, their youngest child, was born in Miami, Oklahoma, in 1927. From 1945 to 1946 he served as a corporal in the U.S. Army Medical Corps. He married Nancy Fortner in 1950, and they reside in Hominy, Oklahoma. They have four children: Kenneth, Cynthia, Robert, and Sandra.

Chinnubbie worked most of his life at Warren Petroleum, where he was traffic manager and taught classes in transportation and traffic management of interstate commerce law. In 1984 he took early retirement from the firm. Chinnubbie was named Transportation Man of the Year by the Delta Nu Alpha Transportation Frater-

Chief Dode McIntosh and his sons; left to right: *Chinnubbie, Nocus H., William V., and Dode, who holds a photograph of his son Waldo E. McIntosh, Jr., who was killed in World War II.*

nity, Tulsa chapter, and has served as president of the Tulsa Transportation Club.

The Creek tribal leaders elected Chinnubbie to the office of district judge of the Creek Nation. He is also on the board of directors of the Creek Nation Community Hospital. Since 1961 Chinnubbie and Nancy have attended the Southside Christian church.

Courtesy McIntosh Family

Daniel Newnan McIntosh (1822–1896), son of Chief William McIntosh

Albert Gallatin McIntosh (1848–1915), son of Daniel Newnan McIntosh

Waldo Emerson ("Dode") McIntosh (1893–   ), principal chief of the Creek Nation, 1961–71, and son of Albert Gallatin McIntosh

Courtesy McIntosh Family

Chief Waldo Emerson ("Dode") McIntosh

APPENDIX III

Text of Treaties between the United States and the Creek Nation

TREATY WITH THE CREEKS, 1805.

A convention between the United States and the Creek Nation of Indians, concluded, at the City of Washington, on the fourteenth day of November, in the year of our Lord one thousand eight hundred and five.

Nov. 14, 1805.

7 Stat., 96.
Proclamation,
June 2, 1806.

ARTICLES of a Convention made between Henry Dearborn, secretary of war, being specially authorized therefor by the President of the United States, and Oche Haujo, William M'Intosh, Tuskenehau Chapce, Tuskenehau, Enehau Thlucco, Checopeheke, Emantlau, chiefs and head men of the Creek nation of Indians, duly authorized and empowered by said nation.

ART. I. The aforesaid chiefs and head men do hereby agree, in consideration of certain sums of money and goods to be paid to the said Creek nation by the government of the United States as hereafter stipulated, to cede and forever quit claim, and do, in behalf of their nation, hereby cede, relinquish, and forever quit claim unto the United States all right, title, and interest, which the said nation have or claim, in or unto a certain tract of land, situate between the rivers Oconee and Ocmulgee (except as hereinafter excepted) and bounded as follows, viz:

Beginning at the high shoals of Apalacha, where the line of the treaty of fort Wilkinson touches the same, thence running in a straight line, to the mouth of Ulcofauhatche, it

Cession by the
Creek Indians.

Boundaries.

113

being the first large branch or fork of the Ocmulgee, above the Seven Islands: *Provided, however,* That if the said line should strike the Ulcofauhatche, at any place above its mouth, that it shall continue round with that stream so as to leave the whole of it on the Indian side; then the boundary to continue from the mouth of the Ulcofauhatche, by the water's edge of the Ocmulgee river, down to its junction with the Oconee; thence up the Oconee to the present boundary at Tauloohatche creek; thence up said creek and following the present boundary line to the first-mentioned bounds, at the high shoals of Apalacha, excepting and reserving to the Creek nation, the title and possession of a tract of land, five miles in length and three in breadth, and bounded as follows, viz: Beginning on the eastern shore of the Ocmulgee river, at a point three miles on a straight line above the mouth of a creek called Oakchoncoolgau, which empties into the Ocmulgee, near the lower part of what is called the old Ocmulgee fields—thence running three miles eastwardly, on a course at right angles with the general course of the river for five miles below the point of beginning;—thence, from the end of the three miles, to run five miles parallel with the said course of the river; thence westwardly, at right angles with the last-mentioned line to the river; thence by the river to the first-mentioned bounds.

A militry post, etc., to be established. And it is hereby agreed, that the President of the United States, for the time being, shall have a right to establish and continue a military post, and a factory or trading house on said reserved tract; and to make such other use of the said tract as may be found convenient for the United States, as long as the government thereof shall think proper to continue the said military post or trading house. And it is also agreed on the part of the Creek nation, that the navigation and fishery of the Ocmulgee, from its junction with the Oconee to the mouth of the Ulcofauhatchee, shall be free to the white people; provided they use no traps for taking fish; but nets and seines may be used, which shall be drawn to the eastern shore only.

United States to have a right to the use of a road to the Mobile. ART. II. It is hereby stipulated and agreed, on the part of the Creek nation that the government of the United States shall forever hereafter have a right to a horse path, through the Creek country, from the Ocmulgee to the Mobile, in such direction as shall, by the President of the United States, be considered most convenient, and to clear out the same, and lay logs over the creeks: And the citizens of said States, shall at all times have a right to pass peaceably on said path, under such regulations and restrictions, as the government of the United States shall from time to time direct; and the Creek chiefs will have boats kept at the several rivers for the conveyance of men and horses, and houses of entertainment established at suitable places on said path for the accommodation of travellers; and the respective ferriages and prices of entertainment for men and horses, shall be regulated by the present agent, Col. Hawkins, or by his successor in office, or as is usual among white people.

Art. III. It is hereby stipulated and agreed, on the part of the United States, as a full consideration for the land ceded by the Creek nation in the first article, as well as by permission granted for a horse path through their country, and the occupancy of the reserved tract, at the old Ocmulgee fields, that there shall be paid annually to the Creek nation, by the United States for the term of eight years, twelve thousand dollars in money or goods, and implements of husbandry, at the option of the Creek nation, seasonably signified from time to time, through the agent of the United States, residing with said nation, to the department of war; and eleven thousand dollars shall be paid in like manner, annually, for the term of the ten succeeding years, making in the whole, eighteen payments in the course of eighteen years, without interest: The first payment is to be made as soon as practicable after the ratification of this convention by the government of the United States, and each payment shall be made at the reserved tract on the Old Ocmulgee fields. *[An annuity to be paid to the Creek nation.]*

Art. IV. And it is hereby further agreed, on the part of the United States, that in lieu of all former stipulations relating to blacksmiths, they will furnish the Creek nation for eight years, with two blacksmiths and two strikers. *[Blacksmiths to be provided at the expense of United States.]*

Art. V. The President of the United States may cause the line to be run from the high shoals of Apalacha, to the mouth of Ulcofauhatche, at such time, and in such manner, as he may deem proper, and this convention shall be obligatory on the contracting parties as soon as the same shall have been ratified by the government of the United States. *[Line to be run at the time, etc., prescribed by the President.]*

Done at the place, and on the day and year above written.

| H. Dearborn, | [L. S.] |
| Oche Haujo, his x mark, | [L. S.] |

115

William McIntosh, his x mark,	[L. S.]
Tuskenehau Chapco, his x mark,	[L. S.]
Tuskenehau, his x mark,	[L. S.]
Enehau Thlucco, his x mark,	[L. S.]
Chekopeheke Emanthau, his x mark,	[L. S.]

Signed and sealed in presence of—

James Madison,
Rt. Smith,
Benjamin Hawkins,
Timothy Barnard,
Jno. Smith,
Andrew McClary.

The foregoing articles have been faithfully interpreted.

Timothy Barnard, interpreter.

TREATY WITH THE CREEKS, 1814.

Aug. 9, 1814.

7 Stat., 120.
Proclamation,
Feb. 16, 1815.

Articles of agreement and capitulation, made and concluded this ninth day of August, one thousand eight hundred and fourteen, between major general Andrew Jackson, on behalf of the President of the United States of America, and the chiefs, deputies, and warriors of the Creek Nation.

WHEREAS an unprovoked, inhuman, and sanguinary war, waged by the hostile Creeks against the United States, hath been repelled, prosecuted and determined, successfully, on the part of the said States, in conformity with principles of national justice and honorable warfare—And whereas consideration is due to the rectitude of proceeding dictated by instructions relating to the re-establishment of peace: Be it remembered, that prior to the conquest of that part of the Creek nation hostile to the United States, numberless aggressions had been committed against the peace, the property, and the lives of citizens of the United States, and those of the Creek nation in amity with her, at the mouth of Duck river, Fort Mimms, and elsewhere, contrary to national faith, and the regard due to an article of the treaty concluded at New-York, in the year seventeen hundred ninety, between the two nations: That the United States, previously to the perpetration of such outrages, did, in order to ensure future amity and concord between the Creek nation and the said states, in conformity with the stipulations of former treaties, fulfil, with punctuality and good faith, her engagements to the said nation: that more than two-thirds of the whole number of chiefs and warriors of the Creek nation, disregarding the genuine spirit of existing treaties, suffered themselves to be instigated to violations of their national honor, and the respect due to a part of their own nation faithful to the United States and the principles of humanity, by impostures [impostors,] denominating themselves Prophets, and by the duplicity and misrepresentation of foreign emissaries, whose governments are at war, open or understood, with the United Sates. Wherefore,

1st—The United States demand an equivalent for all expenses incurred in prosecuting the war to its termination, by a cession of all the territory belonging to the Creek nation within the territories of the United States, lying west, south, and south-eastwardly, of a line to be run and described by persons duly authorized and appointed by the President of the United States—Beginning at a point on the eastern bank of the Coosa river, where the south boundary line of the Cherokee nation crosses the same; running from thence down the said Coosa river with its eastern bank according to its various meanders to a point one mile above the mouth of Cedar creek at Fort Williams, thence east two miles, thence south two miles, thence west to the eastern bank of the said Coosa river, thence down the eastern bank thereof according to its various meanders to a point opposite the upper end of the great falls, (called by the natives Woetumka,) thence east from a true meridian line to a point due north of the mouth of Ofucshee, thence south by a like meridian line to the mouth of Ofucshee on the south side of the Tallapoosa river, thence up the same, according to its various meanders, to a point where a direct course will cross the same at the distance of ten miles from the mouth thereof, thence a direct line to the mouth of Summochico creek, which empties into the Chatahouchie river on the east side thereof below the Eufaulau town, thence east from a true meridian line to a point which shall intersect the line now dividing the lands claimed by the said Creek nation from those claimed and owned by the state of Georgia: Provided, nevertheless, that where any possession of any chief or warrior of the Creek nation, who

Cession of territory by the Creeks as equivalent to the expenses of the war.

shall have been friendly to the United States during the war, and taken an active part therein, shall be within the territory ceded by these articles to the United States, every such person shall be entitled to a reservation of land within the said territory of one mile square, to include his improvements as near the centre thereof as may be, which shall inure to the said chief or warrior, and his descendants, so long as he or they shall continue to occupy the same, who shall be protected by and subject to the laws of the United States; but upon the voluntary abandonment thereof, by such possessor or his descendants, the right of occupancy or possession of said lands shall devolve to the United States, and be identified with the right of property ceded hereby.

Guaranty of other territory of the Creeks.

2nd—The United States will guarantee to the Creek nation, the integrity of all their territory eastwardly and northwardly of the said line to be run and described as mentioned in the first article.

Intercourse with British or Spanish posts to cease.

3d—The United States demand, that the Creek nation abandon all communication, and cease to hold any intercourse with any British or Spanish post, garrison, or town; and that they shall not admit among them, any agent or trader, who shall not derive authority to hold commercial, or other intercourse with them, by licence from the President or authorized agent of the United States.

Establishment of military posts.

4th—The United States demand an acknowledgment of the right to establish military posts and trading houses, and to open roads within the territory, guaranteed to the Creek nation by the second article, and a right to the free navigation of all its waters.

All property taken to be surrendered.

5th—The United States demand, that a surrender be immediately made of all the persons and property, taken from the citizens of the United States, the friendly part of the Creek nation, the Cherokee, Chickesaw, and Choctaw nations, to the respective owners; and the United States will cause to be immediately restored to the formerly hostile Creeks, all the property taken from them since their submission, either by the United States, or by any Indian nation in amity with the United States, together with all the prisoners taken from them during the war.

The prophets and instigators of the war to be given up.

6th—The United States demand the caption and surrender of all the prophets and instigators of the war, whether foreigners or natives, who have not submitted to the arms of the

United States, and become parties to these articles of capitulation, if ever they shall be found within the territory guaranteed to the Creek nation by the second article.

7th—The Creek nation being reduced to extreme want, and not at present having the means of subsistance, the United States, from motives of humanity, will continue to furnish gratuitously the necessaries of life, until the crops of corn can be considered competent to yield the nation a supply, and will establish trading houses in the nation, at the discretion of the President of the United States, and at such places as he shall direct, to enable the nation, by industry and economy, to procure clothing.

Supplies of corn to be presented to the Creeks.

8th—A permanent peace shall ensue from the date of these presents forever, between the Creek nation and the United States, and between the Creek nation and the Cherokee, Chickasaw, and Choctaw nations.

Permanent peace.

9th—If in running east from the mouth of Summochico creek, it shall so happen that the settlement of the Kennards, fall within the lines of the territory hereby ceded, then, and in that case, the line shall be run east on a true meridian to Kitchofoonee creek, thence down the middle of said creek to its junction with Flint River, immediately below the Oakmulgee town, thence up the middle of Flint river to a point due east of that at which the above line struck the Kitchofoonee creek, thence east to the old line herein before mentioned, to wit: the line dividing the lands claimed by the Creek nation, from those claimed and owned by the state of Georgia.

Lines of the territory.

The parties to these presents, after due consideration, for themselves and their constituents, agree to ratify and confirm the preceding articles, and constitute them the basis of a permanent peace between the two nations; and they do hereby solemnly bind themselves, and all the parties concerned and interested, to a faithful performance of every stipulation contained therein.

In testimony whereof, they have hereunto, interchangeably, set their hands and affixed their seals, the day and date above written.

Andrew Jackson, major
  general commanding
  Seventh Military District,   [L. S.]

Tustunnuggee Thlucco,
  speaker for the Upper
  Creeks, his x mark,   [L. S.]

Micco Aupoegau, of Tou-
kaubatchee, his x mark, [L. S.]
Tustunnuggee Hopoiee,
speaker of the Lower
Creeks, his x mark, [L. S.]
Micco Achulee, of Cowe-
tau, his x mark, [L. S.]
Hopoiee Hutkee, of Sou-
wagoolo, his x mark, [L. S.]
Hopoiee Hutkee, for Ho-
poie Yoholo, of Souwo-
goolo, his x mark, [L. S.]
Folappo Haujo, of Eufau-
lau, on Chattohochee,
his x mark, [L. S.]
Pachee Haujo, of Apala-
choocla, his x mark, [L. S.]
Timpoeechee Bernard,
captain of Uchees, his x
mark, [L. S.]
Uchee Micco, his x mark, [L. S.]
Yoholo Micco, of Kiali-
jee, his x mark, [L. S.]
Socoskee Emautla, of
Kialijee, his x mark, [L. S.]
Choocchau Haujo, of
Woccocoi, his x mark, [L. S.]
Esholoctee, of Nauchee,
his x mark, [L. S.]
Yoholo Micco, of Talla-
poosa Eufaulau, his x
mark, [L. S.]
Stinthellis Haujo, of Abe-
coochee, his x mark, [L. S.]
Ocfuskee Yoholo, of Tou-
tacaugee, his x mark, [L. S.]
John O'Kelly, of Coosa, [L. S.]
Eneah Thlucco, of Im-
mookfau, his x mark, [L. S.]
William McIntosh, jr.,
major of Cowetau, his x
mark, [L. S.]

Tuskee Eneah, of Cusse-
tau, his x mark, [L. S.]
Faue Emautla, of Cusse-
tau, his x mark [L. S.]
Toukaubatchee Tustunnug-
gee, of Hitchetee, his x
mark, [L. S.]
Noble Kinnard, of Hitche-
tee, his x mark, [L. S.]
Espokokoke Haujo, of
Wewoko, his x mark, [L. S.]
Eneah Thlucco Hopoiee,
of Talesee, his x mark, [L. S.]
Efau Haujo, of Puccan
Tallahassee, his x mark,[L. S.]
Talessee Fixico, of Ocheo-
bofau, his x mark, [L. S.]
Nomatlee Emautla, or
captain Isaacs, of Cou-
soudee, his x mark, [L. S.]
Tuskegee Emautla, or
John Carr, of Tuskegee,
his x mark, [L. S.]
Alexander Grayson, of
Hillabee, his x mark, [L. S.]
Lowee, of Ocmulgee, his
x mark, [L. S.]
Nocoosee Emautla, of
Chuskee Tallafau, his x
mark, [L. S.]
William McIntosh, for
Hopoiee Hajo, of Oos-
eoochee, his x mark, [L. S.]
William McIntosh, for
Chehahaw Tustunnug-
gee, of Chehahaw, his x
mark, [L. S.]
William McIntosh, for
Spokokee Tustunnug-
gee, of Otellewhoyon-
nee, his x mark, [L. S.]

Done at Fort Jackson, in presence of—

 Charles Cassedy, acting secretary,

 Benjamin Hawkins, agent for Indian affairs,

 Return J. Meigs, A. C. nation,

 Robert Butler, Adjutant General U. S. Army,

 J. C. Warren, assistant agent for Indian affairs,

 George Mayfield,

 Alexander Curnels,

 George Lovett,

Public interpreters.

TREATY WITH THE CREEKS, 1818.

A treaty of limits between the United States and the Creek nation of Indians, made and concluded at the Creek Agency, on Flint river, the twenty-second day of January, in the year of our Lord, one thousand eight hundred and eighteen.

Jan. 22, 1818.

7 Stat., 171.
Proclamation,
Mar. 28, 1818.

JAMES MONROE, President of the United States of America, by David Brydie Mitchell, of the state of Georgia, agent of Indian affairs for the Creek nation, and sole commissioner, specially appointed for that purpose, on the one part, and the undersigned kings, chiefs, head men, and warriors, of the Creek nation, in council assembled, on behalf of the said nation, of the other part, have entered into the following articles and conditions, viz:

ART. 1. The said kings, chiefs, head men, and warriors, do hereby agree, in consideration of certain sums of money to be paid to the said Creek nation, by the government of the United States, as hereinafter stipulated, to cede and forever quit claim, [and do, in behalf of their said nation, hereby cede, relinquish, and forever quit claim,] unto the United States, all right, title, and interest, which the said nation have, or claim, in or unto, the two following tracts of land, situate, lying, and being, within the following bounds; that is to say: 1st. Beginning at the mouth of Goose Creek on the Alatamahau river, thence, along the line leading to the Mounts, at the head of St. Mary's river, to the point where it is intersected by the line run by the commissioners of the

The Creeks cede two tracts of land to United States.

Bounds of the first tract.

United States under the treaty of Fort Jackson, thence, along the said last-mentioned line, to a point where a line, leaving the same, shall run the nearest and a direct course, by the head of a creek called by the Indians Alcasalekie, to the Ocmulgee river; thence, down the said Ocmulgee river, to its junction with the Oconee, the two rivers there forming the Alatamahau; thence, down the Alatamahau, to the first-mentioned bounds, at the mouth of Goose creek. 2d. Beginning at the high shoals of the Appalachee river, and from thence, along the line designated by the treaty made at the city of Washington, on the fourteenth day of November, one thousand eight hundred and *five* [fifteen], to the Ulcofouhatchie, it being the first large branch, or fork, of the Ocmulgee, above the Seven Islands; thence, up the eastern bank of the Ulcofouhatchie, by the water's edge, to where the path, leading from the high shoals of the Appalchie to the shallow ford on the Chatahochie, crosses the same; and, from thence, along the said path, to the shallow ford on the Chatahochie river; thence, up the Chatahochie river, by the water's edge, on the eastern side, to Suwannee old town; thence, by a direct line, to the head of Appalachie; and thence, down the same, to the first-mentioned bounds at the high shoals of Appalachie.

ART. 2. It is hereby stipulated and agreed, on the part of the United States, as a full consideration for the two tracts of land ceded by the Creek nation in the preceding article, that there shall be paid to the Creek nation by the United States, within the present year, the sum of twenty thousand dollars, and ten thousand dollars shall be paid annually for the term of ten succeeding years, without interest; making, in the whole, eleven payments in the course of eleven years, the present year inclusive; and the whole sum to be paid, one hundred and twenty thousand dollars.

ART. 3. And it is hereby further agreed, on the part of the United States, that, in lieu of all former stipulations relating to blacksmiths, they will furnish the Creek nation for three years with two blacksmiths and strikers.

ART. 4. The President may cause any line to be run which may be necessary to designate the boundary of any part of both, or either, of the tracts of land ceded by this treaty, at such time, and in such manner, as he may deem proper. And this treaty shall be obligatory on the contracting parties as

Second tract.

Payment for said cession.

Two blacksmiths and strikers to be furnished.

Line to be run by United States.

Treaty to be obligatory when ratified.

soon as the same shall be ratified by the government of the United States.

Done at the place, and on the day before written.

D. B. Mitchell.

Tustunnugee Thlucco, his x mark,	[L. S.]	Eufaulu Micco, his x mark,	[L. S.]
Tustunnugee Hopoie, his x mark,	[L. S.]	Hopoethle Hauja, his x mark,	[L. S.]
William McIntosh,	[L. S.]	Hopoie Hatkee, his x mark,	[L. S.]
Tuskeenchaw, his x mark,	[L. S.]		
Hopoie Haujo, his x mark,	[L. S.]	Yoholo Micco, his x mark,	[L. S.]
Cotchau Haujo, his x mark,		Tustunnugee, his x mark,	[L. S.]
Inthlansis Haujo, his x mark,	[L. S.]	Fatuske Henehau, his x mark,	[L. S.]
Cowetau Micco, his x mark,	[L. S.]	Yauhau Hqaujo, his x mark,	[L. S.]
Cusselau Micco, his x mark,	[L. S.]	Tuskeegee Emautla, his x mark,	[L. S.]
		Tustunnugee Hoithleloeo, his x mark,	[L. S.]

Present:

D. Brearly, colonel Seventh Infantry.

Wm. S. Mitchell, assistant agent, I. A. C. N.

M. Johnson, lieutenant corps of artillery.

Sl. Hawkins,

George [G. L.] Lovet,

Interpreters

TREATY WITH THE CREEKS, 1821.

Articles of a treaty entered into at the Indian Spring, in the Creek Nation, by Daniel M. Forney, of the State of North Carolina; and David Meriwether, of the State of Georgia, specially appointed for that purpose, on the part of the United States; and the Chiefs, Head Men, and Warriors, of the Creek Nation, in council assembled.

Jan. 8, 1821.

7 Stat., 215.
Proclamation,
Mar. 2, 1821.

Cession by the Creek.

ART. 1. The Chiefs, Head Men, and Warriors, of the Creek Nation, in behalf of the said nation, do, by these presents, cede to the United States all that tract or parcel of land, situate, lying, and being, east of the following bounds and

Boundaries.

limits, viz: Beginning on the east bank of Flint river, where Jackson's line crosses, running thence, up the eastern bank of the same, along the water's edge, to the head of the principal western branch; from thence, the nearest and a direct line, to the Chatahooche river, up the eastern bank of the said river, along the water's edge, to the shallow Ford, where the present boundary line between the state of Georgia and the

Proviso.

Creek nation touches the said river: *Provided, however,* That, if the said line should strike the Chatahooche river, below the Creek village Buzzard-Roost, there shall be a set-off made so as to leave the said village one mile within the Creek nation; excepting and reserving to the Creek nation the title and possession, in the manner and form specified, to all the land hereafter excepted, viz: one thousand acres, to be laid off in a square, so as to include the Indian Spring in the centre thereof; as, also, six hundred and forty acres on the western bank of the Oakmulgee river, so as to include the improvements at present in the possession of the Indian Chief General M'Intosh.

Title of certain tracts to be in the Creek nation, so long as the occupants remain, etc.

ART. 2. It is hereby stipulated, by the contracting parties, that the title and possession of the following tracts of land shall continue in the Creek nation so long as the present occupants shall remain in the personal possession thereof, viz: one mile square, each, to include, as near as may be, in the centre thereof, the improvements of Michey Barnard, James Barnard, Buckey Barnard, Cussena Barnard, and Efauemathlaw, on the east side of Flint river; which reservations shall constitute a part of the cession made by the first article, so soon as they shall be abandoned by the present occupants.

Reservation for United States agency.

ART. 3. It is hereby stipulated, by the contracting parties, that, so long as the United States continue the Creek agency at its present situation on Flint river, the land included within the following boundary, viz: beginning on the east bank of Flint river, at the mouth of the Boggy Branch, and running out, at right angles, from the river, one mile and a half; thence up, and parallel with, the river, three miles: thence, parallel with the first line, to the river; and thence, down the river, to the place of beginning; shall be reserved to the Creek nation for the use of the United States' agency, and shall constitute a part of the cession made by the first article, whenever the agency shall be removed.

ART. 4. It is hereby stipulated and agreed, on the part of the United States, as a consideration for the land ceded by the Creek nation by the first article, that there shall be paid to the Creek nation, by the United States, ten thousand dollars in hand, the receipt whereof is hereby acknowledged; forty thousand dollars as soon as practicable after the ratification of this convention: five thousand dollars, annually, for two years thereafter; sixteen thousand dollars, annually, for five years thereafter; and ten thousand dollars, annually, for six years thereafter; making, in the whole, fourteen payments in fourteen successive years, without interest, in money or goods and implements of husbandry, at the option of the Creek nation, reasonably signified, from time to time, through the agent of the United States residing with said nation, to the Department of War. And, as a further consideration for said cession, the United States do hereby agree to pay to the state of Georgia whatever balance may be found due by the Creek nation to the citizens of said state, whenever the same shall be ascertained, in conformity with the reference made by the commissioners of Georgia, and the chiefs, head men, and warriors, of the Creek nation, to be paid in five annual instalments without interest, provided the same shall not exceed the sum of two hundred and fifty thousand dollars; the commissioners of Georgia executing to the Creek nation a full and final relinquishment of all the claims of the citizens of Georgia against the Creek nation, for property taken or destroyed prior to the act of Congress of one thousand eight hundred and two, regulating the intercourse with the Indian tribes.

Payment for lands ceded.

United States to pay to the State of Georgia the balance due by the Creek Nation.

ART. 5. The President of the United States shall cause the line to be run from the head of Flint river to the Chatahooche river, and the reservations made to the Creek nation to be laid off, in the manner specified in the first, second, and third, articles of this treaty, at such time and in such manner as he may deem proper, giving timely notice to the Creek nation; and this Convention shall be obligatory on the contracting parties, as soon as the same shall have been ratified by the government of the United States.

The President to cause the line to be run, etc.

Done at the Indian Spring, this eighth day of January, A. D. eighteen hundred and twenty-one.

D. M. Forney,	[L. S.]	Taskagee Emauthlau, his x	
D. Meriwether,	[L. S.]	mark,	[L. S.]
Wm. McIntosh,	[L. S.]	Tuckle Luslee, his x mark,	[L. S.]
Tustunnugee Hopoie, his x		Tuckte Lusttee Haujo, his	
mark,	[L. S.]	x mark,	[L. S.]
Efau Emauthlau, his x		Cunepee Emauthlau, his x	
mark,	[L. S.]	mark,	[L. S.]
Holoughlan, or Col. Blue,		Hethlepoie, his x mark,	[L. S.]
his x mark,	[L. S.]	Tuskeenaheocki, his x	
Cussetau Micco, his x		mark,	[L. S.]
mark,	[L. S.]	Chaughle Micco, his x	
Sotetan Haujo, his x		mark,	[L. S.]
mark,	[L. S.]	Isfaune Tustunnuggee	
Etomme Tustunnuggee,		Haujo, his x mark,	[L. S.]
his x mark,	[L. S.]	Wau Thlucco Haujo, his x	
Itchu Haujo, his x mark,	[L. S.]	mark,	[L. S.]
Alabama Tustunnuggee,		Houpauthlee Tustunnug-	
his x mark,	[L. S.]	gee, his x mark,	[L. S.]
Holoughlan Tustunnug-		Nenehaumaughtoochie,	
gee, his x mark,	[L. S.]	his x mark,	[L. S.]
Auhauluck Yohola, his x		Henelau Tixico, his x	
mark,	[L. S.]	mark,	[L. S.]
Oseachee Tustunnuggee,		Tusekeagh Haujo, his x	
his x mark,	[L. S.]	mark,	[L. S.]
		Joseph Marshall,	[L. S.]

In presence of—
I. McIntosh,
David Adams,
Daniel Newman,
      Commissioners of Georgia.
D. B. Mitchell, Agent for I. A.
William Meriwether, secretary U. S. C.
William Cook, secretary C. G.
William Hambly,
Sl. Hawkins,
George Levett,

      Interpreters.

TREATY WITH THE CREEKS, 1821.

Articles of agreement entered into, between the undersigned Commissioners, appointed by the Governor of the state of Georgia, for and on behalf of the citizens of the said state, and the Chiefs, Head Men, and Warriors, of the Creek nation of Indians.

Jan. 8, 1821.

7 Stat., 217.
Proclamation,
Mar. 2, 1821.

WHEREAS, at a conference opened and held at the Indian Spring, in the Creek nation, the citizens of Georgia, by the aforsaid commissioners, have represented that they have claims to a large amount against the said Creek nation of Indians: Now, in order to adjust and bring the same to a speedy and final settlement, it is hereby agreed by the aforesaid commissioners, and the chiefs, head men, and warriors, of the said nation, that all the talks had upon the subject of these claims at this place, together with all claims on either side, of whatever nature or kind, prior to the act of Congress of one thousand eight hundred and two, regulating the intercourse with the Indian tribes, with the documents in support of them, shall be referred to the decision of the President of the United States, by him to be decided upon, adjusted, liquidated, and settled, in such manner, and under such rules, regulations, and restrictions, as he shall prescribe: *Provided, however,* if it should meet the views of the President of the United States, it is the wish of the contracting parties, that the liquidation and settlement of the aforesaid claims shall be made in the state of Georgia, at such place as he may deem most convenient for the parties interested, and the decision and award, thus made and rendered, shall be binding and obligatory upon the contracting parties.

Claims on either side referred to decision of the President. 1802, ch. 13.

Proviso.

In witness whereof, we have hereunto set our hands and seals, this eighth day of January, one thousand eight hundred and twenty-one.

J. McIntosh,	[L. S.]
David Adams,	[L. S.]
Daniel Newman,	[L. S.]
William McIntosh,	[L. S.]
Tustunnuggee Hopoie, his x mark,	
	[L. S.]
Efau Emauthlau, his x mark,	[L. S.]

Present:

D. M. Forney,
D. Meriwether.

Jan. 8, 1821.

DISCHARGE FOR ALL CLAIMS ON THE CREEKS.

Whereas a treaty or convention has this day been made and entered into, by and between the United States and the Creek nation, by the provisions of which the United States have agreed to pay, and the commissioners of the state of Georgia have agreed to accept, for and on behalf of the citizens of the state of Georgia, having claims against the Creek nation, prior to the year one thousand eight hundred and two, the sum of two hundred and fifty thousand dollars:

Commissioners of Georgia release the Creeks from all claims prior to 1802.

Now, know all men by these presents, that we, the undersigned, commissioners of the state of Georgia, for, and in consideration of, the aforesaid sum of two hundred and fifty thousand dollars, secured by the said treaty or convention to be paid to the state of Georgia, for the discharge of all bona fide and liquidated claims, which the citizens of the said state may establish against the Creek nation, do, by these presents, release, exonerate, and discharge, the said Creek nation from all and every claim and claims, of whatever description, nature, or kind, the same may be, which the citizens of Georgia now have, or may have had, prior to the year one thousand eight hundred and two, against the said nation. And we

Claims transferred to United States.

do hereby assign, transfer, and set over, unto the United States, for the use and benefit of the said Creek nation, for the consideration hereinbefore expressed, all the right, title, and interest, of the citizens of the said state, to all claims, debts, damages, and property, of every description and denomination, which the citizens of the said state have, or had, prior to the year one thousand eight hundred and two, as aforesaid, against the said Creek nation.

In witness whereof, we have hereunto affixed our hands and seals, at the Mineral Spring, in the said Creek nation, this eighth day of January, one thousand eight hundred and twenty-one.

J. McIntosh,	[L. S.]
David Adams,	[L. S.]
Daniel Newman,	[L. S.]

Present:

    D. M. Forney,

    D. Meriwether,

    D. B. Mitchell, Agent for Indian Affairs.

TREATY WITH THE CREEKS, 1825.

Articles of a convention, entered into and concluded at the Indian Springs, between Duncan G. Campbell, and James Meriwether, Commissioners on the part of the United States of America, duly authorised, and the Chiefs of the Creek Nation, in Council assembled.

Feb. 12, 1825.

7 Stat., 237
Proclamation,
Mar. 7, 1825.

WHEREAS the said Commissioners, on the part of the United States, have represented to the said Creek Nation that it is the policy and earnest wish of the General Government, that the several Indian tribes within the limits of any of the states of the Union should remove to territory to be designated on the west side of the Mississippi river, as well for the better protection and security of said tribes, and their improvement in civilization, as for the purpose of enabling the United States, in this instance, to comply with the compact entered into with the State of Georgia, on the twenty-fourth day of April, in the year one thousand eight hundred and two: And the said Commissioners having laid the late Message of the President of the United States, upon this subject, before a General Council of said Creek Nation, to the end that their removal might be effected upon terms advantageous to both parties:

Preamble.

And whereas the Chiefs of the Creek Towns have assented to the reasonableness of said proposition, and expressed a willingness to emigrate beyond the Mississippi, *those of Tokaubatchee excepted:*

These presents therefore witness, that the contracting parties have this day entered into the following Convention:

ART. 1. The Creek nation cede to the United States all the lands lying within the boundaries of the State of Georgia, as

Cession by the Creek.

defined by the compact hereinbefore cited, now occupied by said Nation, or to which said Nation have title or claim; and also, all other lands which they now occupy, or to which they have title or claim, lying north and west of a line to be run from the first principal falls upon the Chatauhoochie river, above Cowetau town, to Ocfuskee Old Town, upon the Tallapoosa, thence to the falls of the Coosaw river, at or near a place called the Hickory Ground.

Further agreement between the contracting parties.

ART. 2. It is further agreed between the contracting parties, that the United States will give, in exchange for the lands hereby acquired, the like quantity, acre for acre, westward of the Mississippi, on the Arkansas river, commencing at the mouth of the Canadian Fork thereof, and running westward between said rivers Arkansas and Canadian Fork, for quantity. But whereas said Creek Nation have considerable improvements within the limits of the territory hereby ceded, and will moreover have to incur expenses in their removal, it is further stipulated, that, for the purpose of rendering a fair equivalent for the losses and inconveniences which said Nation will sustain by removal, and to enable them to obtain supplies in their new settlement, the United States agree to pay to the Nation emigrating from the lands herein ceded, the sum of four hundred thousand dollars, of which amount there shall be paid to said party of the second part, as soon as practicable after the ratification of this treaty, the sum of two hundred thousand dollars. And as soon as the said party of the second part shall notify the Government of the United States of their readiness to commence their removal, there shall be paid the further sum of one hundred thousand dollars. And the first year after said emigrating party shall have settled in their new country, they shall receive of the amount first above named, the further sum of twenty-five thousand dollars. And the second year, the sum of twenty-five thousand dollars. And annually, thereafter, the sum of five thousand dollars, until the whole is paid.

Annuities to be equally divided.

ART. 3. And whereas the Creek Nation are now entitled to annuities of thirty thousand dollars each, in consideration of cessions of territory heretofore made, it is further stipulated that said last mentioned annuities are to be hereafter divided in a just proportion between the party emigrating and those that may remain.

Territory offered said Indians to be explored, etc.

ART. 4. It is further stipulated that a deputation from the said parties of the second part, may be sent out to explore the territory herein offered them in exchange; and if the same be not acceptable to them, then they may select any other territory, west of the Mississippi, on Red, Canadian, Arkansas, or Missouri Rivers—the territory occupied by the Cherokees and Choctaws excepted; and if the territory so to be selected shall be in the occupancy of other Indian tribes, then the United States will extinguish the title of such occupants for the benefit of said emigrants.

ART. 5. It is further stipulated, at the particular request of the said parties of the second part, that the payment and disbursement of the first sum herein provided for, shall be made by the present Commissioners negotiating this treaty. *Payment of the first sum to be made by the commissioners.*

ART. 6. It is further stipulated, that the payments appointed to be made, the first and second years, after settlement in the West, shall be either in money, merchandise, or provisions, at the option of the emigrating party. *Other payments.*

ART. 7. The United States agree to provide and support a blacksmith and wheelwright for the said party of the second part, and give them instruction in agriculture, as long, and in such manner, as the President may think proper. *Provision to be made by United States.*

ART. 8. Whereas the said emigrating party cannot prepare for immediate removal, the United States stipulate, for their protection against the incroachments, hostilities, and impositions, of the whites, and of all others; but the period of removal shall not extend beyond the first day of September, in the year eighteen hundred and twenty-six. *Extension of the time of their removal, etc.*

ART. 9. This treaty shall be obligatory on the contracting parties, so soon as the same shall be ratified by the President of the United States, by and with the consent of the Senate thereof. *When to take effect.*

In testimony whereof, the commissioners aforesaid, and the chiefs and head men of the Creek nation, have hereunto set their hands and seals, this twelfth day of February, in the year of our Lord one thousand eight hundred and twenty-five.

Duncan G. Campbell,	[L. S.]	Athlan Hajo, his x mark,	[L. S.]
James Meriwether,	[L. S.]	Tuskenahah, his x mark,	[L. S.]
Commissioners on the		Benjamin Marshall,	[L. S.]
part of the United		Cocous Hajo, his x mark,	[L. S.]
States.		Forshatepu Mico, his x	
William McIntosh, head		mark,	[L. S.]
chief of Cowetaus,	[L. S.]	Oethlamata Tustunnuggee,	
Chilly McIntosh,	[L. S.]	his x mark,	[L. S.]
Joseph Marshall,	[L. S.]	Tallasee Hajo, his x mark,	[L. S.]

Tuskegee Tustunnuggee,
his x mark,   [L. S.]
Foshajee Tustunnuggee,
his x mark,   [L. S.]
Emau Chuccolocana, his x
mark,   [L. S.]
Abeco Tustunnuggee, his
x mark,   [L. S.]
Hijo Hajo, his x mark,   [L. S.]
Thla Tho Hajo, his x
mark,   [L. S.]
Tomico Holueto, his x
mark,   [L. S.]
Yah Te Ko Hajo, his x
mark,   [L. S.]
No cosee Emautla, his x
mark,   [L. S.]
Col. Wm. Miller,
Thleeatchea, his x
mark,   [L. S.]
Abeco Tustunnuggee, his
x mark,   [L. S.]
Hoethlepoga Tustunnug-
gee, his x mark,   [L. S.]
Hepocokee Emautla, his x
mark,   [L. S.]
Samuel Miller, his x
mark,   [L. S.]
Tomoc Mico, his x mark,   [L. S.]
Charles Miller, his x
mark,   [L. S.]
Tallasee Hoja, or John
Carr, his x mark,   [L. S.]
Otulga Emautla, his x
mark,   [L. S.]
Ahalaco Yoholo of Cuse-
tau, his x mark,   [L. S.]
Walucco Hajo, of New
Yauco, his x mark,   [L. S.]
Etommee Tustunnuggee,
of Cowetau, his x mark,   [L. S.]

Holahtau, or Col. Blue,
his x mark,   [L. S.]
Cowetau Tustunnuggee,
his x mark,   [L. S.]
Artus Mico, or Roby Mc-
Intosh, his x mark,   [L. S.]
Cohausee Ematla, of New
Yauco, his x mark,   [L. S.]
Nineomau Tochee, of
New Yauco, his x mark, [L. S.]
Konope Emautla, Sand
Town, his x mark,   [L. S.]
Chawacala Mico, Sand
Town, his x mark,   [L. S.]
Foctalustee Emaulta, Sand
Town, his x mark,   [L. S.]
Josiah Gray, from Hitcha-
tee, his x mark,   [L. S.]
William Kannard, from
Hitchatee, his x mark,   [L. S.]
Neha Thlucto Hatkee,
from Hitchatee, his x
mark,   [L. S.]
Halathla Fixico, from Big
Shoal, his x mark,   [L. S.]
Alex. Lasley, from Talle-
dega, his x mark,   [L. S.]
Espokoke Hajo, from Tal-
ledega, his x mark,   [L. S.]
Emauthla Hajo, from Tal-
ledega, his x mark,   [L. S.]
Nincomatachee, from Tal-
ledega, his x mark,   [L. S.]
Chuhah Hajo, from Talle-
dega, his x mark,   [L. S.]
Efie Ematla, from Talle-
dega, his x mark,   [L. S.]
Atausee Hopoie, from Tal-
ledega, his x mark,   [L. S.]
James Fife, from Talle-
dega, his x mark,   [L. S.]

Executed on the day as above written, in presence of—

John Crowell, agent for Indian affairs,

Wm. F. Hay, secretary,

Wm. Meriwether,

Wm. Hambly, United States interpreter.

———

Whereas, by a stipulation in the Treaty of the Indian Springs, in 1821, there was a reserve of land made to include the said Indian Springs for the use of General William M'Intosh, be it therefore known to all whom it may concern, that we, the undersigned chiefs and head men of the Creek nation, do hereby agree to relinquish all the right, title, and control of the Creek nation to the said reserve, unto him the said William M'Intosh and his heirs, forever, as in full and ample a manner as we are authorized to do.

July 25, 1825.

Big B. W. Warrior,	[L. S.]
Yoholo Micco, his x mark,	[L. S.]
Little Prince, his x mark,	[L. S.]
Hopoie Hadjo, his x mark,	[L. S.]
Tuskehenahau, his x mark,	[L. S.]
Oakefuska Yohola, his x mark,	[L. S.]
John Crowell, agent for Indian affairs,	[L. S.]

July 25, 1825.

———

Whereas the foregoing articles of convention have been concluded between the parties thereto: And, whereas, the Indian Chief, General William McIntosh, claims title to the Indian Spring Reservation (upon which there are very extensive buildings and improvements) by virtue of a relinquishment to said McIntosh, signed in full council of the nation: And, whereas the said General William McIntosh hath claim to another reservation of land on the Ocmulgee river, and by his lessee and tenant, is in possession thereof:

Feb. 14, 1825.

Additional article.

Now these presents further witness, that the said General William McIntosh, and also the Chiefs of the Creek Nation, in council assembled, do quit claim, convey, and cede to the

United States, the reservations aforesaid, for, and in consideration of, the sum of twenty-five thousand dollars, to be paid at the time and in the manner as stipulated, for the first instalment provided for in the preceding treaty. Upon the ratification of these articles, the possession of said reservations shall be considered as passing to the United States, and the accruing rents of the present year shall pass also.

In testimony whereof, the said commissioners, on the part of the United States, and the said William McIntosh, and the chiefs of the Creek nation, have hereunto set their hands and seals, at the Indian Springs, this fourteenth day of February, in the year of our Lord one thousand eight hundred and twenty-five.

Duncan G. Campbell,	[L. S.]
James Meriwether,	[L. S.]
	United States commissioners.
William McIntosh,	[L. S.]
Eetommee Tustunnuggee, his x mark,	[L. S.]
Tuskegoh Tustunnuggee, his x mark,	[L. S.]
Cowetau Tustunnuggee, his x mark,	[L. S.]
Col. Wm. Miller, his x mark,	[L. S.]
Josiah Gray, his x mark,	[L. S.]
Nehathlucco Hatchee, his x mark,	[L. S.]
Alexander Lasley, his x mark,	[L. S.]
William Canard, his x mark,	[L. S.]

Witnesses at execution:
Wm. F. Hay, secretary,
Wm. Hambly, United States interpreter.

TREATY WITH THE CREEKS, 1826.

Jan. 24, 1826.
7 Stat., 286.
Proclamation,
Apr. 22, 1826.

Articles of a treaty made at the City of Washington, this twenty-fourth day of January, one thousand eight hundred and twenty-six, between James Barbour, Secretary of War, thereto specially authorized by the President of the United States, and the undersigned, Chiefs and Head Men of the Creek Nation of Indians, who have received full power from the said Nation to conclude and arrange all the matters herein provided for.

WHEREAS a treaty was concluded at the Indian Springs, on the twelfth day of February last, between Commissioners on the part of the United States, and a portion of the Creek Nation, by which an extensive district of country was ceded to the United States.

And whereas a great majority of the Chiefs and Warriors of the said Nation have protested against the execution of the said Treaty, and have represented that the same was signed on their part by persons having no sufficient authority to form treaties, or to make cessions, and that the stipulations in the said Treaty are, therefore, wholly void.

And whereas the United States are unwilling that difficulties should exist in the said Nation, which may eventually lead to an intestine war, and are still more unwilling that any cessions of land should be made to them, unless with the fair understanding and full assent of the Tribe making such cession, and for a just and adequate consideration, it being the policy of the United States, in all their intercourse with the Indians, to treat them justly and liberally, as becomes the relative situation of the parties.

Now, therefore, in order to remove the difficulties which have thus arisen, to satisfy the great body of the Creek nation, and to reconcile the contending parties into which it is unhappily divided, the following articles have been agreed upon and concluded, between James Barbour, Secretary of War, specially authorized as aforesaid, and the said Chiefs and Head Men representing the Creek Nation of Indians:

ARTICLE 1.

The Treaty concluded at the Indians Springs, on the twelfth day of February, one thousand eight hundred and twenty-five, between Commissioners on the part of the United States and the said Creek Nation of Indians, and ratified by the United States on the seventh day of March, one thousand eight hundred and twenty-five, is hereby declared to be null and void, to every intent and purpose whatsoever; and every right and claim arising from the same is hereby cancelled and surrendered.

Treaty of Indian Springs declared null and void.

ARTICLE 2.

Lands ceded to
the United States.

The Creek Nation of Indians cede to the United States all the land belonging to the said Nation in the State of Georgia, and lying on the east side of the middle of the Chatahoochie river. And, also, another tract of land lying within the said State, and bounded as follows: Beginning at a point on the western bank of the said river, forty-seven miles below the point where the boundary line between the Creeks and Cherokees strikes the Chatahoochie river, near the Buzzard's Roost, measuring the said distance in a direct line, and not following the meanders of the said river; and from the point of beginning, running in a direct line to a point in the boundary line, between the said Creeks and the Cherokees, thirty miles west of the said Buzzard's Roost; thence to the Buzzard's Roost, and thence with the middle of the said river to the place of beginning.

ARTICLE 3.

Payment to said
nation.

Immediately after the ratification of this Treaty, the United States agree to pay to the Chiefs of the said Nation the sum of two hundred and seventeen thousand six hundred dollars to be divided among the Chiefs and Warriors of the said Nation.

ARTICLE 4.

Perpetual annuity.

The United States agree to pay to the said Nation an additional perpetual annuity of twenty thousand dollars.

ARTICLE 5.

Difficulties to
be adjusted, etc.

The difficulties which have arisen in the said nation, in consequence of the Treaty of the Indian Springs, shall be amicably adjusted, and that portion of the Creek Nation who signed that treaty shall be admitted to all their privileges, as members of the Creek Nation, it being the earnest wish of the United States, without undertaking to decide upon the complaints of the respective parties, that all causes of dissatisfaction should be removed.

ARTICLE 6.

That portion of the Creek Nation, known as the friends and followers of the late General William McIntosh, having intimated to the government of the United States their wish to remove west of the Mississippi, it is hereby agreed, with their assent, that a deputation of five persons shall be sent by them, at the expense of the United States, immediately after the ratification of this treaty, to examine the Indian country west of the Mississippi, not within either of the States or Territories, and not possessed by the Choctaws or Cherokees. And the United States agree to purchase for them, if the same can be conveniently done upon reasonable terms, wherever they may select, a country, whose extent shall, in the opinion of the President, be proportioned to their numbers. And if such purchase cannot be thus made, it is then agreed that the selection shall be made where the President may think proper, just reference being had to the wishes of the emigrating party.

A deputation to examine the Indian country west of the Mississippi, etc.

ARTICLE 7.

The emigrating party shall remove within twenty-four months, and the expense of their removal shall be defrayed by the United States. And such subsistence shall also be furnished them, for a term not exceeding twelve months after their arrival at their new residence, as, in the opinion of the President, their numbers and circumstances may require.

Emigrating party to remove within twenty-four months, etc.

ARTICLE 8.

An agent, or sub-agent and Interpreter, shall be appointed to accompany and reside with them. And a blacksmith and wheelwright shall be furnished by the United States. Such assistance shall also be rendered to them in their agricultural operations, as the President may think proper.

An agent, etc., to be appointed to reside with them.

ARTICLE 9.

In consideration of the exertions used by the friends and followers of General McIntosh to procure a cession at the Indian Springs, and of their past difficulties and contemplated

Presents to Indians.

137

removal, the United States agree to present to the Chiefs of the party, to be divided among the Chiefs and Warriors, the sum of one hundred thousand dollars, if such party shall amount to three thousand persons, and in that proportion for any smaller number. Fifteen thousand dollars of this sum to be paid immediately after the ratification of this treaty, and the residue upon their arrival in the country west of the Mississippi.

ARTICLE 10.

Certain damages to be ascertained, etc.

It is agreed by the Creek Nation, that an agent shall be appointed by the President, to ascertain the damages sustained by the friends and followers of the late General McIntosh, in consequence of the difficulties growing out of the Treaty of the Indian Springs, as set forth in an agreement entered into with General Gains, at the Broken Arrow,[a] and which have been done contrary to the laws of the Creek Nation; and such damages shall be repaired by the said Nation, or the amount paid out of the annuity due to them.

ARTICLE 11.

Commissioners to value improvements.

All the improvements which add real value to any part of the land herein ceded shall be appraised by Commissioners, to be appointed by the President; and the amount thus ascertained shall be paid to the parties owning such improvements.

ARTICLE 12.

Possession of country ceded.

Possession of the country herein ceded shall be yielded by the Creeks on or before the first day of January next.

ARTICLE 13.

Guarantee by United States.

The United States agree to guarantee to the Creeks all the country, not herein ceded, to which they have a just claim,

---

[a]This agreement, which is unratified, is set forth in the Appendix, post, p. 1034. The original can not be found, but a copy is among the files of the Indian Office, General Files, Creek, 1825–1826.— E. P. Gaines.

and to make good to them any losses they may incur in consequence of the illegal conduct of any citizen of the United States within the Creek country.

ARTICLE 14.

The President of the United States shall have authority to select, in some part of the Creek country, a tract of land, not exceeding two sections, where the necessary public buildings may be erected, and the persons attached to the agency may reside.

Authority of the President.

ARTICLE 15.

Wherever any stream, over which it may be necessary to establish ferries, forms the boundary of the Creek country, the Creek Indians shall have the right of ferriage from their own land, and the citizens of the United States from the land to which the Indian title is extinguished.

Liberty granted the Creeks.

ARTICLE 16.

The Creek Chiefs may appoint three Commissioners from their own people, who shall be allowed to attend the running of the lines west of the Chatahoochy river, and whose expenses, while engaged in this duty, shall be defrayed by the United States.

Commissioners to attend the running of the lines.

ARTICLE 17.

This treaty, after the same has been ratified by the President and Senate, shall be obligatory on the United States and on the Creek nation.

Treaty binding when ratified.

In testimony whereof, the said James Barbour, Secretary of War, authorized as aforesaid, and the chiefs of the said Creek nation of Indians, have hereunto set their hands, at the City of Washington, the day and year aforesaid.

James Barbour,

O-poth-le Yoholo, his x mark,

John Stidham, his x mark,

Mad Wolf, his x mark,

Menawee, his x mark,

Tuskeekee Tustunnuggee, his x mark,

Charles Cornells, his x mark,

Timpoochy Barnard, his x mark,

Apauly Tustunnuggee, his x mark,

Coosa Tustunnuggee, his x mark,   Ledagi, his x mark,
Nahetluc Hopie, his x mark,   Yoholo Micco, his x mark.
Selocta, his x mark,

In presence of—
Thomas L. McKenney,
Lewis Cass,
John Crowell, agent for Indian Affairs,
Hezekiah Miller,
John Ridge, secretary Creek delegation,
David Vann.

Mar. 31, 1826.

7 Stat., 289.

SUPPLEMENTARY ARTICLE TO THE CREEK TREATY OF THE TWENTY-FOURTH JANUARY, 1826.

WHEREAS a stipulation in the second article of the Treaty of the twenty-fourth day of January, 1826, between the undersigned, parties to said Treaty, provides for the running of a line "beginning at a point on the western bank of the Chatahoochee river, forty-seven miles below the point where the boundary line between the Creeks and Cherokees strikes the said river, near the Buzzard's Roost, measuring the said distance in a direct line, and not following the meanders of the said river, and from the point of beginning, running in a direct line to a point in the boundary line between the said Creeks and the Cherokees, thirty miles west of the said Buzzard's Roost, thence to the Buzzard's Roost, and thence with the middle of said river to the place of beginning." And whereas it having been represented to the party to the said Treaty in behalf of the Creek Nation, that a certain extension of said lines might embrace in the cession all the lands which will be found to lie within the chartered limits of Georgia, and which are owned by the Creeks, the undersigned do hereby agree to the following extension of said lines, viz: In the place of "forty-seven miles," as stipulated in the second article of the Treaty aforesaid, as the point of beginning, the undersigned agree that it shall be *fifty* miles, in a direct line below the point designated in the second article of said Treaty; thence running in a direct line to a point in the boundary line between the Creeks and Cherokees, *forty-five miles*

Further cession.

west of said Buzzard's Roost, in the place of "thirty miles," as stipulated in said Treaty; thence to the Buzzard's Roost, and thence to the place of beginning—it being understood that these lines are to stop at their intersection with the boundary line between Georgia and Alabama, wherever that may be, if that line shall cross them in the direction of the Buzzard's Roost, at a shorter distance than it is provided they shall run; and provided, also, that if the said dividing line between Georgia and Alabama shall not be reached by the extension of the two lines aforesaid, the one three, and the other fifteen miles, they are to run and terminate as defined in this supplemental article to the Treaty aforesaid.

It is hereby agreed, in consideration of the extension of said lines, on the part of the other party to the Treaty aforesaid, in behalf of the United States, to pay to the Creek Nation, immediately upon the ratification of said Treaty, the sum of thirty thousand dollars. *Payment to Creeks.*

In witness whereof, the parties aforesaid have hereunto set their hands and seals, this thirty-first day of March, in the year of our Lord one thousand eight hundred twenty-six.

James Barbour,	[L. S.]
Opothle Yoholo, his x mark,	[L. S.]
John Stidham, his x mark,	[L. S.]
Mad Wolf, his x mark,	[L. S.]
Tuskeekee Tustunnuggee, his x mark,	[L. S.]
Yoholo Micco, his x mark,	[L. S.]
Menawee, his x mark,	[L. S.]
Charles Cornells, his x mark,	[L. S.]
Apauly Tustunnuggee, his x mark,	[L. S.]
Coosa Tustunnuggee, his x mark,	[L. S.]
Nathetluc Hopie, his x mark,	[L. S.]
Selocta, his x mark,	[L. S.]
Timpoochy Barnard, his x mark,	[L. S.]
Ledagi, his x mark,	[L. S.]

In presence of—

Thomas L. McKenney,
John Crowell, agent for Indian affairs,
John Ridge, secretary,
David Vann,
Wm. Hambly.

TREATY WITH THE CREEKS, 1827.

Nov. 15, 1827.

7 Stat., 307.
Proclamation,
Mar 4, 1828.

Articles of agreement made and concluded at the Creek Agency, on the fifteenth day of November, one thousand eight hundred and twenty-seven, between Thomas L. McKenney, and John Crowell, in behalf of the United States, of the one part, and Little Prince and others, Chiefs and Head Men of the Creek Nation, of the other part.

Object of the treaty.

WHEREAS a Treaty of Cession was concluded at Washington City in the District of Columbia, by JAMES BARBOUR, Secretary of War, of the one part, and OPOTHLEOHOLO, JOHN STIDHAM, and OTHERS, of the other part, and which Treaty bears date the twenty-fourth day of January, one thousand eight hundred and twenty-six; and whereas, the object of said Treaty being to embrace a cession by the Creek Nation, of all the lands owned by them within the chartered limits of Georgia, and it having been the opinion of the parties, at the time when said Treaty was concluded, that all, or nearly all, of said lands were embraced in said cession, and by the lines as defined in said Treaty, and the supplemental article thereto: and whereas it having been since ascertained that the said lines in said Treaty, and the supplement thereto, do not embrace all the lands owned by the Creek Nation within the chartered limits of Georgia, and the President of the United States having urged the Creek nation further to extend the limits as defined in the Treaty aforesaid, and the Chiefs and head men of the Creek Nation being desirous of complying with the wish of the President of the United States, therefore, they, the Chiefs and head men aforesaid, agree to cede, and they do hereby cede to the United States, all the remaining lands now owned or claimed by the Creek Nation, not heretofore ceded, and which, on actual survey, may be found to lie within the chartered limits of the State of Georgia.

United States agree to pay $27,491.

In consideration whereof, and in full compensation for the above cession, the undersigned, THOMAS L. McKENNEY, and JOHN CROWELL, in behalf of the United States, do hereby agree to pay to the Chiefs and head men of the Creek Nation aforesaid, and as soon as may be after the approval and ratification of this agreement, in the usual forms, by the President and Senate of the United States, and its sanction by a council of the Creek Nation, to be immediately convened for the purpose, or by the subscription of such names, in addition to those subscribed to this instrument, of Chiefs and head men of the nation, as shall constitute it the act of the Creek Nation—the sum of twenty-seven thousand four hundred and ninety-one dollars.

It is further agreed by the parties hereto, in behalf of the United States, to allow, on account of the cession herein made, the additional sum of fifteen thousand dollars, it being the understanding of both the parties, that five thousand dollars of this sum shall be applied, under the direction of the President of the United States, towards the education and support of Creek children at the school in Kentucky, known by the title of the "*Chocktaw Academy,*" and under the existing regulations; also, one thousand dollars towards the support of the Withington, and one thousand dollars towards the support of the Asbury stations, so called, both being schools in the Creek Nation, and under regulations of the Department of War; two thousand dollars for the erection of four horse mills, to be suitably located under the direction of the President of the United States; one thousand dollars to be applied to the purchase of cards and wheels, for the use of the Creeks, and the remaining five thousand dollars, it is agreed, shall be paid in blankets and other necessary and useful goods, immediately after the signing and delivery of these presents.

Further agreement.

In witness whereof, the parties have hereunto set their hands and seals, this fifteenth day of November, one thousand eight hundred and twenty-seven.

Thomas L. McKenney,	[L. S.]
John Crowell,	[L. S.]
Little Prince, his x mark,	[L. S.]
Epau-emathla, his x mark,	[L. S.]
Timpouchoe Burnard, his x mark,	[L. S.]
Hathlan Haujo, his x mark,	[L. S.]
Oke-juoke Yau-holo, his x mark,	[L. S.]
Cassetaw Micco, his x mark,	[L. S.]

In presence of—

Luther Blake, secretary,
Andrew Hamill,
Whitman C. Hill,
Thomas Crowell.

Whereas, the above articles of agreement and cession were entered into at the Creek agency on the day and date therein mentioned, between the Little Prince, the head man of the nation, and five other chiefs, and Thomas L. McKenney and John Crowell, commissioners on the part of the United States, for the cession of all the lands owned or claimed by the Creek nation, and not heretofore ceded, and which, on actual survey, may be found to lie within the chartered limits of the State of Georgia, and which said agreement was made subject to the approval and ratification by the President and Senate of the United States, and the approval and sanction of the Creek nation, in general council of the said nation.

Now, these presents witnesseth, that we, the undersigned, chiefs and head men of the Creek nation in general council convened, at *Wetumph,* the third day of January, one thousand eight hundred and twenty-eight, have agreed and stipulated with John Crowell, commissioner on the part of the United States, for and in consideration of the additional sum of five thousand dollars, to be paid to us in blankets, and other necessary articles of clothing, immediately after the signing and sealing of these presents, to sanction, and by these presents do hereby approve, sanction, and ratify, the abovementioned and foregoing articles of agreement and session.

In witness whereof, the parties have hereunto set their hands and seals, the day and date above mentioned.

John Crowell,	[L. S.]	Cowetaw Micco, his x	
Broken Arrow Town:		mark,	[L. S.]
Little Prince, his x mark,	[L. S.]	Oswichu Town:	
Tuskugu, his x mark,	[L. S.]	Halatta Tustinuggu, his x	
Cotche Hayre, his x mark,	[L. S.]	mark,	[L. S.]
Cusetau Town:		Octiatchu Emartla, his x	
Tukchenaw, his x mark,	[L. S.]	mark,	[L. S.]
Epi Emartla, his x mark,	[L. S.]	Charles Emartla, his x	
Oakpushu Yoholo, his x		mark,	[L. S.]
mark,	[L. S.]	Uchee Town:	
Cowetau Town:		Timpoeche Barned, his x	
Neah Thleuco, his x		mark,	[L. S.]
mark,	[L. S.]	Chawaccola Hatchu	
Tomasa Town:		Town:	
Colitchu Ementla, his x		Coe E. Hayo, his x mark,	[L. S.]
mark,	[L. S.]	Powas Yoholo, his x	
Arthlau Hayre, his x		mark,	[L. S.]
mark,	[L. S.]	Ema Hayre, his x mark,	[L. S.]

In presence of—
Luther Blake, secretary,
Andrew Hamill,
Enoch Johnson,
Thomas Crowell.
Benjamin Marshall,
Paddy Carr,
    interpreters.
Joseph Marshall,
John Winslett.

NOTES

Chapter 1
The Birth of McIntosh

1. Rudyard Kipling, "The Ballad of the East and West," in *Bartlett's Familiar Quotations* (Boston: Little, Brown & Co., 1975), p. 872.

2. Harriet Turner Corbin, *A History and Genealogy of Chief William McIntosh, Jr., and His Known Descendants,* edited by Carl C. Burdick, Sr. (Long Beach, Calif.: n.p., n.d.), p. 12. Cited hereafter as *Corbin;* Margaret Mackintosh of Mackintosh, *The History of the Clan Mackintosh and the Clan Chattan.* Revised and updated by Lachlan Mackintosh of Mackintosh. Midlothian, Scotland: Macdonald Publishers, 1982), pp. 2–3.

3. Bessie Lewis, *They Called Their Town Darien: Being a Short History of Darien and McIntosh County, Georgia* (Darien, Ga.: Darien News, 1975), p. 19.

4. Corbin, p. 23.

5. Tradition. This information comes from the McIntosh tradition today and is not to be found in a book or article (cited hereafter as *Tradition*).

6. Sturge's Map of 1818, Surveyor's Office, Georgia Department of Archives and History, Atlanta, Georgia.

7. Corbin, p. 23.

8. Tradition.

9. Major Caleb Swan, United States Army, *A Visit to the Creek Nation in 1790: Journal of Major C. Swan,* Horseshoe Bend National Military Park, Daviston, Alabama. Cited hereafter as *Swan.*

10. Tradition. Chief (Ret) W. E. McIntosh's son, Chinnubbie, has given background information on today's traditional ceremonies among the Creeks.

11. John R. Swanton, "Creek Social Organization and Social Usages of the Indians of the Creek Confederacy," in *42nd Annual Report, 1924–1925* (Washington, D.C.: Bureau of American Ethnology, 1928), pp. 174–91, 446–70.

12. Tradition.

13. Tradition.

14. Corbin, pp. 23–24.

15. Lewis, p. 36.

16. Lewis, p. 37.

17. Swan, p. 30. This practice was current at least until 1791. It may still have been in effect when McIntosh was chosen a chief of Coweta-Cussetta, about 1800.

18. James C. Bonner, "The Family Relationship of Chief William McIntosh," *Carroll County Historical Quarterly* 1, no. 2 (Spring/Summer 1968): 35.

19. *United States 19th Congress, 2nd Session: House Reports, #98, Select Committee on Georgia, Relative to the Creek Indian Lands,* compiled by Edward Everette (Washington, D.C.: Gales & Seaton, 1827), p. 809 (cited hereafter as *House Reports*).

20. Swan, p. 12.

21. *House Reports,* pp. 809–10.

22. Corbin, p. 24.

23. *House Reports,* p. 90.

24. James C. Bonner, "Tustunuge Hutke and Creek Factionalism on the Georgia-Alabama Frontier," *The Alabama Review* (April 1957), p. 121.

25. Helen Todd, *Tomochichi: Indian Friend of the Georgia Colony* (Atlanta: Cherokee Publishing Co., 1977), p. 18.

Chapter 2
The Red Sticks' War
1813–14

1. Charles Kappler, comp. and ed., *Indian Affairs: Laws and Treaties, Vol. II* (Washington, D.C.: Government Printing Office, 1903), pp. 85–86.

2. H. S. Halbert and T. H. Ball, *The Creek War of 1813 and 1814,* edited by Frank L. Owsley, Jr. (Auburn: University of Alabama Press, 1969), p. 36.

3. Halbert and Ball, p. 62.

4. Halbert and Ball, p. 85.

5. Thomas S. Woodward, *Woodward's Reminiscences of the Creek, or Muscogee, Indians, Containing Letters to Friends in Georgia and Alabama* (Montgomery, Ala.: Barrett & Wimbish, 1859), p. 32.

6. James C. Bonner, "William McIntosh," in *Georgians in Profile: Historical Essays in Honor of Ellis Merton Coulter,* edited by Horace Montgomery (Athens: University of Georgia Press, 1958), p. 120.

7. Bonner, "Tustunuge Hutke," p. 123.

8. Halbert and Ball, p. 89.

9. Halbert and Ball, p.134.

10. Halbert and Ball, pp. 246, 275.

11. R. S. Cotteril, *The Southern Indians: The Story of the Civilized Tribes before Removal* (Norman: The University of Oklahoma Press, 1954), p. 185.

12. Corbin, p. 49.

13. James W. Holland, *Andrew Jackson and the Creek War: Victory at Horseshoe* (Auburn: University of Alabama Press, 1968), p. 18.

14. Holland, p. 27.

15. Woodward, p. 101.

16. Holland, p. 37.

17. Correspondence, General Jackson to Secretary of War John Armstrong, Fort Williams, 2 April 1814, *Jackson Papers,* 1st Series, Vol. 19, Document #1608 (cited hereafter as *Jackson Papers*).

18. Claimants Account Book, "Claims against Hostile Creek Indians," The Norwood Indian Springs Collection, Georgia Department of Archives and History, Atlanta.

19. Holland, p. 38.

20. Papers of Admiral the Honorable Sir Alexander Forrester Inglis Cochrane, National Library of Scotland, Edinburgh, Scotland.

21. Letters from General McIntosh to D. B. Mitchell, Indian Agent, Telemon Cuyler Collection, University of Georgia, Athens (cited hereafter as Letters).

22. Letters, 13 April 1818.

23. Letters, 13 April 1818.

24. Cotteril, p. 220.

Chapter 3
Georgia's Push for the Removal of All Indians

1. Angie Debo, *The Road to Disappearance* (Norman: University of Oklahoma Press, 1941), p. 84.

2. *House Reports,* p. 342.

3. John Clarke, *Consideration on the Purity of the Principles of William H. Crawford* (Printed at the Georgia Advertising Office, 1819), p.

131, as quoted in Antonio J. Waring's *Laws of the Creek Nation*, University of Georgia Libraries, Miscellaneous Publications No. 1 (Athens: University of Georgia Press, 1960), p. 3.

4. Debo, p. 85.
5. Kappler, p. 155.
6. Letters, 15 June 1818.
7. Debo, p. 87.
8. Corbin, p. 48.
9. Convention between Creek and Cherokee Indians at Acorn Bluff, Creek Indian Nation, Treaty of 11 January 1821. 53–2 File II, Creek Indians, Georgia Department of Archives and History, Atlanta.
10. Kappler, p. 204.
11. *House Reports*, pp. 332–333.
12. *House Reports*, pp. 55, 342.
13. *House Reports*, pp. 638–639.
14. *House Reports*, pp. 451–452.
15. Debo, pp. 87–88.
16. *House Reports*, p. 90.
17. *House Reports*, p. 319.
18. *House Reports*, p. 332.
19. *House Reports*, p. 317.
20. *House Reports*, p. 419.
21. *House Reports*, p. 332.
22. *House Reports*, p. 90.
23. *House Reports*, p. 260.
24. Corbin, p. 32.
25. *Georgia: The Murder of General William McIntosh. Treaties of Indian Springs 1821–1825. Also Report of Joseph Vallance Bevan. Letters, Treaties, Executive Reports and the Trial of John Crowell, Indian Agent*, p. 201, Georgia Department of Archives and History, Atlanta. Cited hereafter as *Georgia*.
26. *Georgia*, p. 201.
27. Kappler, p. 214.
28. R. J. Massey, "Thrilling Story of the McIntosh Assassination by Creek Nation Is Reviewed by Dr. Massey," *Atlanta Constitution*, Sunday, November, no year.
29. Kappler, p. 532.
30. Kappler, p. 583.
31. Kappler, p. 583.
32. Kappler, p. 583.
33. *House Reports*, p. 325.
34. *House Reports*, p. 318.
35. *House Reports*, p. 7.

36. Memorial of the Creek Chiefs to the Georgia Legislature, 12 April 1825, *Creek Letters,* Georgia Department of Archives and History, Atlanta.

37. *House Reports,* pp. 151–52, 578, 382.

38. *House Reports,* pp. 327, 87.

Chapter 4
The Death of McIntosh

1. George White, "General William McIntosh," in *Historical Collections of Georgia* (New York: Pudney & Russell, 1855), pp. 170–73, quoting Albert James Pickett. Most of this chapter is based on the recounting of Jim Hutton's father-in-law, as told to Pickett; that recounting is probably the most accurate.

2. White, p. 172.

3. Corbin, p. 35.

Chapter 5
The Creeks Move West

1. Corbin, p. 33.

2. Corbin, p. 33.

3. Woodward, p. 55.

4. Debo, p. 51.

5. Woodward, p. 148.

Appendix I

1. *Georgia Journal,* 28 April 1818, Georgia Department of Archives and History, Atlanta.

2. Bonner, "Georgians in Profile," p. 126.

3. See Waring, *Laws of the Creek Nation.*

INDEX

ABOUT THE AUTHOR

GEORGE CHAPMAN was born on March 16, 1928, in Greenville, South Carolina, the son of Zena and Judson Chapman. In 1946 he enlisted in the Navy and served for two years. After returning to Greenville, he attended Furman University, from which he was graduated in 1951 with a major in English.

Having felt a calling to the ministry, George then entered Southern Baptist Theological Seminary in Louisville, Kentucky. Following graduation from seminary in 1954, he volunteered as a chaplain in the U.S. Army and was stationed in Germany. After his tour of duty he returned to seminary for further study in the field of pastoral counseling. In 1959 he was called to be pastor of Sandy Springs Baptist church near Pelzer, South Carolina.

After a brief pastoral career, George moved to Atlanta and worked for Capitol Records and managed radio station WOMN in Decatur, Georgia. In 1970 he entered graduate school at West Georgia College in Carrollton to study psychology. It was there, while pursuing his degree, that he learned of an "Indian treasure." The real treasure turned out to be the story of Chief William McIntosh.

Following a decade as a counselor with the Fulton County Department of Human Resources, George resigned his position and became a freelance writer. This is his first book.

George and his wife, Shirley, live in Atlanta.